TEACHERS TALK

ABOUT TEACHING

TEACHERS TALK

ABOUT TEACHING

Coping with change in

turbulent times

edited by
Judith Bell

OPEN UNIVERSITY PRESS
Buckingham • Philadelphia

Open University Press
Celtic Court
22 Ballmoor
Buckingham
MK18 1XW

and

1900 Frost Road, Suite 101
Bristol, PA 19007, USA

First Published 1995

A catalogue record of this book is available from the British Library

ISBN   0 335 19174 6 (pb)

Library of Congress Cataloging-in-Publication Data
Teachers talk about teaching: coping with change in turbulent times /
edited by Judith Bell.
p.   cm.
Includes bibliographical references and index.
ISBN 0–335–19174–6 (pbk.)
1. Teachers—Great Britain—Attitudes. 2. Teaching.
3. Educational change—Great Britain. 4. School management and
organization—Great Britain. 5. Education and state—Great Britain.
I. Bell, Judith, 1930–   .
LB1775.4.G7T436 1995
371.1′00941—dc20   94–25719 CIP

Typeset by Graphicraft Typesetters Ltd, Hong Kong
Printed in Great Britain by St Edmundsbury Press Ltd,
Bury St Edmunds, Suffolk

CONTENTS

CONTRIBUTORS

Dr Judith Bell is a writer, lecturer and consultant and holds honorary fellowships in the Universities of Lancaster, Sheffield and Warwick.

Dr Ken Bryan is principal lecturer in Education at Chester College of Higher Education.

Rosemary Chapman is in her first year as a teacher in a small primary school. She completed a BEd degree at the age of 40, having spent 12 years at home caring for her five children.

Karen Cowley is deputy head of a comprehensive school in Lancashire.

Dr Ann Hanson is staff tutor in education at the Open University in the North West. She has taught in schools, colleges of further education and a former polytechnic.

Jill Horder has taught in four schools and is now head of department of a large high school. She is on the editorial board of the *Journal of Teacher Development*.

Gill Richardson taught in a college of further education and several schools. She was head of sixth form and head of department in her last school, from which she recently took early retirement.

John Ross is deputy head of a school in Eastbourne. He was formerly director of music at a high school in the north of England.

Andrew Spencer is head of the Faculty of Humanities in a Roman Catholic high school. Before that, he held posts as a teacher and head of department of drama and English in various schools.

Peter Swientozielskyj is head of department in a comprehensive school which came into being as a result of LEA reorganizations, school closures and mergers.

Lorna Unwin is a lecturer in post-16 education and training at the University of Sheffield – a post she previously held at the Open University. She has taught in further and adult education and worked as a training consultant in both the public and private sectors.

Stephen Waters is deputy Director of English in a large high school in the North West. He was previously head of department of drama in a 11–16 school in the South West of England.

INTRODUCTION

The idea for this book came originally from discussions with teachers who were attending courses leading to postgraduate degrees in education in several universities. All are, or were, committed teachers who were feeling dismayed at the effect some of the reforms were having on colleagues, pupils and themselves, and concerned at repeated criticisms of teachers which came at regular intervals from various Secretaries of State and from sections of the media. All made a conscious decision to enter the teaching profession and, in spite of the pressures, most have chosen to stay in it.

Their views on the impact of some of the government initiatives provide an insight into what it is like to work in schools today. They have seen fundamental changes, many of which have been welcomed, but the speed with which some legislation has been introduced has left little time for preparation and reflection.

The contributors to the book examine government-initiated reforms which in their view have brought about significant changes in the classroom and the ethos of school life. They consider the impact of the National Curriculum, new criteria for assessment, career prospects, the changed role and influence of governors and the increased workload of teachers. They reflect on changes in conditions of service, the influence of local management of schools (LMS) and the stress felt by many teachers at having to cope with change overload.

All have become keenly aware of the fact that their interpretation of autonomy and professionalism differs significantly from that of some ministers and administrators and this has caused them to examine what autonomy and professionalism really mean for teachers today and in the future – if anything.

Their experience leads most to the conclusion that much good may come from some of the reforms but they make a compelling case for slowing down the rate of change and thorough evaluation of what has been achieved so far (and what has failed) before further reforms are introduced. If that is not done, they feel costly mistakes will be made which will inevitably have far-reaching effects on teachers and pupils. Teachers will continue to leave the profession in increasing numbers, levels of stress will rise and it will be difficult for morale and motivation to be maintained. What is clear is that heads of schools will need to have outstanding qualities of leadership if those who are required to deliver the curriculum and to implement all the changes are to survive.

This book was not intended to be a work of scholarship. Contributors were asked to write about how they felt about being a teacher or to give accounts of their observation of the effects of certain legislation on teachers, particularly in relation to changes introduced as a result of the Education Reform Act of 1988. This they have done, and I am grateful to them for their frankness. They have done their best to present an unbiased account of events as they saw them, though inevitably their accounts are heavily influenced by their own experiences. It could not be otherwise. Even so, I am confident that teachers will see in these chapters similarities to their own situation and will share many of the concerns expressed here.

Part one

CHANGING TEACHING

1

TEACHERS COPING

WITH CHANGE

Judith Bell

Concern about the quality of education provided in our schools was the subject of public and private debate long before the Education Reform Act of 1988 reached the statute book. Prime Ministers and Secretaries of State came and went: periodically statements were made about the state of our public education service and demands were made for improvement. Teachers' organizations were themselves concerned about poor performance in some areas, particularly in those characterized by high levels of social and economic disadvantage. More resources were demanded in order to provide better staffing ratios and improved buildings and equipment. Government demanded greater commitment from teachers. Working parties were convened, reports produced, reforms proposed and rejected and throughout the discussions, teachers held fast to their rights to exercise professional autonomy. They asserted that they were the experts and should be allowed to get on with the job without interference. Well-qualified, competent and committed teachers had throughout their teaching career cherished the right to decide how and in some cases what they should teach – and there are many examples of high quality teaching achieved without any need for external control. The very best teachers demonstrated daily their right to professional autonomy and the freedom this autonomy gave them to identify the best approaches to encourage pupil learning.

Reports by Her Majesty's Inspectors of Schools (HMIs) provide ample evidence of the existence of such teachers. The best were very good but it would be folly to suggest that all teachers achieved such exemplary standards.

By the mid-1970s, public concern had accelerated. Disturbing evidence from HMIs and from public inquiries indicated that all was not well. The much publicized case of the William Tyndale school, which resulted in a public enquiry, highlighted ways in which weak management can, albeit exceptionally, result in something approaching chaos. Robin Auld (1976), the Queen's Counsel who conducted the William Tyndale enquiry on behalf of the Inner London Education Authority, presented a dismal picture of lack of planning and preparation, defects in the structure of curriculum initiatives, lack of co-ordination, poor systems of recording and monitoring, and inadequate management.

The report of this enquiry provided rich pickings for a government determined to take action to improve the quality of education in our schools; in fact knowledge of the ways in which the school had been allowed to operate were of equal concern to many teachers. All branches of the media joined in the condemnation of a local education authority (LEA) which could allow such a breakdown to occur, and of the teachers, several of whom had done their utmost for the pupils in what must have been extraordinarily difficult circumstances. At that time, reports of biased curricula and left-wing orthodoxies being pedalled in the classroom were common and demands for more control and better value for money in education accelerated. We were repeatedly reminded that 'Education, like any other public service, is answerable to the society which it serves and which pays for it' (DES 1977a).

Looking back, central government's move towards greater control was probably inevitable. The message was that if teachers and LEAs could not put their own house in order, then the government would. However, the extent of the control and the ways in which control was seized, were far greater than could have been imagined.

Anxieties about teachers' loss of professional autonomy recur in several chapters and demonstrate the concern felt about increased central government control. The authors are not looking back nostalgically to an imagined golden age when all teachers could do as they liked and be accountable to no-one. They are seriously concerned that the new controls may destroy their ability to make informed decisions about teaching and learning strategies which are in the best interests of the pupils. There have always been controls of course, as Jill Horder points out in Chapter 2. She writes that 'structure, authority and leadership were always needed: but the recent sea-change of public opinion against education has once more laid bare the basic employer–employee nexus, as the very ground shifts under teachers' feet and they are forced to reconsider their aims and purposes'.

Karen Cowley follows a similar line of argument in Chapter 3 when she questions whether accountability to the taxpayer can be congruent with an individual teachers' responsibility to the taught. She clearly thinks it cannot. No-one would question the need to spend money wisely and to be accountable for our actions, but the question is, accountable to whom and for what? In other words, who is laying down the rules and are those rules designed to improve the quality of education or merely to ensure that the costs of education are kept to a minimum, regardless of need. She pleads for a better balance to be achieved between professional and economic accountability and reminds us that 'personal responsibility towards pupils cannot be ensured through legislation, but it is a key factor at all levels of an organization if that organization is to be responsive and effective'.

One of the first major changes initiated by central government, and one which was welcomed in principle, came with the ending of the double examination system of the General Certificate of Education (GCE) O Level and the Certificate of Secondary Education (CSE). This double system had resulted in some cases in crazy double entries so that pupils could, though perhaps exceptionally, take 15 or more external examinations. Examination results were important, even in the days before league tables and so schools hedged their bets. If students failed O Level, they just might get a Grade 1 in CSE, which was credited as being the equivalent of an O Level pass. The double examination meant double standards and employers knew, or thought they knew, which counted for something – and which did not. Teachers' associations and unions, the Schools Council and locally convened working groups had been grappling with the O Level/CSE divide for years and had never been able to agree about ways in which the system could be rationalized, so perhaps it was understandable that the then Secretary of State, Sir Keith Joseph, lost patience and decreed that O Level and CSE would go and that the General Certificate of Secondary Education (GCSE) would take their place.

The timescale for the radical new system was too short, there was insufficient money to buy textbooks and in some subject areas necessary support materials were delayed. However, once the hastily introduced and under-resourced GCSE had settled, most teachers cautiously welcomed the new system, in spite of the work involved in coping with the continuous assessment. They felt it to be a fairer

and more realistic way of testing pupils' achievements. Gradually,
resources were built up, criteria for grading continuous assessment
refined, and teachers and pupils began to settle into the new system.
However, in 1991, only five years after GCSE was introduced, much
of what teachers, pupils and parents felt to be good about the new
system was fundamentally changed. An investigation carried out by
a team of HMIs had reported weaknesses in teacher assessment of
course work and although their findings were strongly contested,
the report gave government the evidence they needed to introduce
a major review of the GCSE. The examination component was
strengthened, the course work component drastically reduced and
the clear inferences which emerged from this action were that teachers just could not be entrusted with the responsible task of making
accurate judgements about the quality of course work produced by
pupils. This incensed teachers. Gill Richardson, in Chapter 7 makes
the point that English teachers in particular have always been accustomed to course work assessment. She admits that they often complained about the amount of time they had to spend on the unpaid
moderation of several hundred folders of work each year, but she
recalls that 'both as a Head of Department and as a Moderator
visiting schools in the Manchester area, I was always impressed by
the meticulous care that was taken over the exercise'. Both she and
Stephen Waters (Chapter 12) felt then, and still feel strongly now,
that for the vast majority of students, continuous assessment ensured that results were achieved which not only reflected pupils'
abilities, but also their commitment to the subject.

The GCSE changes were just the start. Far more radical reforms
were on the way and teachers had barely recovered from one innovation than they were embroiled in the next, and the next, and the
next. It became clear that successive Secretaries of State were determined to lay down the rules and to insist that teachers worked
within frameworks established through a whole sequence of Acts of
Parliament.

The Education Act of 1986 and the Education Reform Act of 1988
heralded an unprecedented series of reforms, the most far-reaching
of which involved the establishment of a National Curriculum. This
was not unexpected and in principle was not as hotly opposed as
some of the other, far more controversial elements. Eric Bolton (1993),
who was Senior Chief Inspector of Her Majesty's Inspectorate in the
1980s felt that:

By 1988, and the Education Reform Act, there was a consensus
about the need for a National Curriculum; that it should be
broad, balanced and relevant, and that what was assessed should

be determined by commonly agreed curricular programmes and goals.

Several of the contributors to this book agree that Eric Bolton's judgement seemed sound. Stephen Waters' view was that 'there was much in the National Curriculum that matched our notion of good practice', but he adds 'there were also serious anomalies, particularly in the assessment process'.

It was when the detail of the National Curriculum became known that serious reservations began to be expressed and in practically all cases criticisms centred around the proposed assessment arrangements. The *Guardian* of 14 December 1993 commented on 'the stupidity of divorcing teaching and assessment' and 'the mess of the National Curriculum and the associated system of testing'. Consensus about the need for a National Curriculum there may have been – in principle – but when the implications became known, the stress levels of teachers required to deliver what proved to be a prescriptive and overcrowded curriculum rose.

Many felt they were not only being told *what* to teach but *how* to teach it. Views varied as to the amount of freedom teachers had and they ranged from the view that they would no longer be in a position to innovate or to devise appropriate methods, to the belief that no matter what the government said, once they were in the classroom, they would be able to make their own decisions about the best ways of managing the learning process. Tony Becher (1989) was confident that 'a large area of discretion remains to the teaching staff', but many contributors to this book would challenge that assertion. Once the 'Orders', issued by the Secretary of State were published, and attainment targets, programmes of study and assessment arrangements made clear, the rules were laid down and teachers had little choice but to implement them – until the publication of the Orders for Key Stage 3 English appeared. English teachers felt this was the last straw. The National Curriculum introduced the notion of age-related key stages (Stage 1 at age 7; 2 at age 11; 3 at age 14 and 4 at age 16). The intention was that standard assessment tests would be set at the end of each key stage so that checks could be made nationally on children's levels of attainment. Chapter 12 provides a graphic account of the events leading up to the teachers' boycott in 1993. In spite of threats of legal action and dismissal issued by the Secretary of State to LEAs, teachers, heads and governors, 99 per cent of teachers declined to carry out the tests. Their refusal to administer the Key Stage 3 tests in 1993, mentioned by several authors in this book as being the turning point in the war of attrition between teachers and the Secretary of State demonstrated the anger, frustration and solidarity of teachers in a way never before experienced.

It is perhaps not surprising that the majority of the publicity and concern about the National Curriculum has centred around the core subjects, but teachers concerned with careers education (placed in what Lorna Unwin in Chapter 11 describes as 'the ambiguous classification of a cross-curricular theme') found themselves faced with different but equally taxing problems. Cross-curricular themes were expected to be 'infused' into all the main subjects of the curriculum. As Watts (1994) says, 'this is fine, in theory. But in practice, it is very difficult to deliver effectively. A lot of support is needed. Little or none has been provided.'

The cross-curricular teachers feel as strongly as other teachers about the tasks they are expected to carry out with little financial or other support. Inevitably, the success of teaching depends on the efforts individual teachers are prepared to put into the job. For some years, funding and support through the Technical and Vocational Education Initiative (TVEI) enabled them to expand work-experience programmes, develop Records of Achievement, and carry out a great deal of curriculum development work. TVEI is due to end in 1997 and, as Watts (1994) points out, 'there is no sign of any comparable initiative to sustain its impact'.

It is likely to take some time – probably years – for the National Curriculum and its assessment to shake down into a fully co-ordinated system, with all implications considered and an appropriate strategy fully tested and refined in the light of experience. Then, there should be a National Curriculum which works in the best interests of the pupils and which makes life possible for those required to deliver it.

I have concentrated so far on the introduction of the National Curriculum and its associated assessment strategy, but as Eric Bolton (1993) indicates, there was even less agreement about other parts of the Education Reform Act.

That is not surprising, given that Local Management of Schools (LMS), open enrolment and grant maintained schools were part of the government's determination to create some of the conditions of a market in education. As such they were products of the Thatcher government's macro-political philosophy: they were political acts of faith. There is nothing wrong with that, but they were not the outcome of long running education debate.

The Local Management in Schools Initiative (LMS) was designed not only to give schools more control over their affairs but also to ensure they planned their activities within their allocated budget. That again seemed to be a good idea in principle in the way that the National Curriculum was a good idea in principle, and many schools have enjoyed the freedom LMS has given them. Some actually report budget surpluses which have enabled them to provide extra facilities and additional support for children. But, as Eric Bolton says, the introduction of LMS was not really 'the outcome of long running education debate'. Pilot schemes were carried out, but fundamental flaws in the system have remained which in some cases have imposed major burdens on schools and their staff and governors. Peter Swientozielskyj (Chapter 9) and Ann Hanson (Chapter 10) describe some of the problems they encountered wholly or partly as a result of LMS, and the efforts they and their colleagues have made to live within the constraints of what they discovered to be an inadequate budget.

It would be easy for critics to infer that these schools were badly managed and that their budgetary control mechanisms were inadequate, but both contributors present an alternative scenario in which unavoidable expenditure, such as teachers' salaries and essential repairs amounted to a sum greater than the total budget. What to do then? All possible economy measures had been taken, and they looked forward with dread to the possibility of yet more redundancies, reorganizations or closures. Financial worries have forced one of the schools to seek a way out of their difficulties by applying for grant maintained status. At one time, staff had no desire to opt out of LEA control, but their financial position became so bad that they could see no alternative.

The crises which staff of both these schools have experienced can be imagined and the reports of early retirements and stress-related illnesses should sound warning bells for any employing body. Studies of occupational stress among headteachers have revealed worrying evidence of job dissatisfaction, general ill health and low morale (Cole and Walker 1989; Cooper and Kelly 1993; Kyriacou 1989; Travers and Cooper 1991). An increasing number of formerly committed teachers are looking forward longingly to the day when they can apply for early retirement. Gill Richardson in Chapter 7 provides an account of why she could no longer face teaching – and yet reports of her qualities as a teacher indicate that she was successful, knowledgeable, up to date in her specialist subject and very experienced in the requirements of the job. In other words, she was a good teacher and the profession cannot afford to lose teachers of quality.

The Cooper and Kelly (1993) study just pre-dates the implementation of the Education Reform Act (ERA) of 1988 and the authors recognize that:

the impact of developments such as the National Curriculum, Local Management of Schools, assessment and testing arrangements, and open enrolment is likely to have been a severe 'gearing up' of the occupational stressors of head teachers, principals and directors. Such changes of role and function, at such a rapid rate, are already showing that the levels of stress damage in the occupational group indicated in this article may be by now only the tip of a much larger iceberg.

If some teachers and heads were suffering from stress and job dissatisfaction before ERA, there is now plenty of evidence that the 'gearing-up' process is well under way. Cooper and Kelly suggest two broad strategies, namely:

> first, there should be major structural approaches to occupational stress management which encompass the employment and selection process, professional and managerial support and recovery programmes, and job design changes; secondly, consideration needs to be given to the public education system, and the demands put upon it, so that the service specification takes into account the human factor.

There is little sign that government has taken much account of 'the human factor'. Gill Richardson gave up the unequal struggle and other contributors to this book have confessed they have had enough and would retire if they were old enough to qualify for early retirement pensions. Andrew Spencer (Chapter 5), who has no desire to turn his back on teaching, nevertheless acknowledges 'there is an ambivalent relationship between change and career' and 'involvement in the management of change can suffer a decrease in commitment if there is too much change or the change is unpopular'. There seems little doubt that many of the changes introduced in recent years have been unpopular. Andrew Spencer discusses some possible coping strategies but if the present and future Secretaries of State continue to reform and to make changes at the speed experienced in recent years, it is difficult to see how even the most sophisticated coping strategies can do much to raise morale and enable teachers to do their work with commitment and enthusiasm.

However, not all is gloom and doom in education. John Ross (Chapter 6), who recently achieved his goal of gaining a deputy headship, looks forward to developing his expertise in senior management and has every intention of remaining in teaching for the whole of his professional life as long as he continues to enjoy the job and as long as he feels positive developments are taking place. He set himself the target of achieving promotion and went for it. He was not looking for power, but for the opportunity to influence the development of his school. He looks forward positively to the future.

Applications for BEd and Post-graduate Certificate in Education (PGCE) courses exceed the number of available places. When the Open University devised a part-time PGCE course in 1994, there was overwhelming demand, particularly for primary places. These mature applicants were making a considered career move and should make a valuable contribution to the teaching force.

Rosemary Chapman (Chapter 4) gained a first-class BEd degree when she was 40 and is now in her first teaching job. She finds it demanding, but she is enjoying the work and looks forward to becoming more expert and to establishing good relationships with the children. She gives us a personal view of the way her BEd prepared her for life in the classroom and her concerns about classroom management and discipline. It is interesting to note that she was unwilling to express her worries to staff of the schools where she carried out teaching practice in case it seemed she was unable to cope. Ken Bryan (Chapter 8) an experienced teacher and college lecturer raises similar issues but his experience and confidence have allowed him to discuss his concerns with colleagues. He writes that he now conceptualizes classroom discipline and control as school issues – they are no longer private concerns. He reflects on changes in his experience of teaching from the end of the 1950s, when his career began, to the present. He concludes by saying, 'For me, professional knowledge is constantly being re-created. If I lose my sensitivity to the processes of re-creation then I shall cease to be a competent teacher, let alone a thinking one'.

Sadly, some teachers now feel that they are so bruised by constant changes which have to be implemented at a speed, allowing no time for reflection, that they probably have lost their sensitivity to the processes of re-creation. A worrying number make it clear they no longer wish to be promoted. The weight of responsibility and the change overload which has proved too much for some teachers is, they feel, probably even worse for headteachers and their deputies.

So far, there are no indications that the demands made on members of the teaching profession are decreasing. The recommendations for the streamlining of the National Curriculum and a more rational approach to assessment produced by Sir Ron Dearing in 1993 should go some way to easing some of the burdens, in particular those associated with the slimming down of the curriculum at all stages. This has been a start, and the recommendations have been cautiously welcomed by the majority of teachers. Sir Ron listened to what teachers were saying and appears to have done his best to remove the worst excesses of the National Curriculum and the associated assessment requirements. One of the most welcome features of the review has been that he not only listened, but he actually thanked teachers for their help – something they are not accustomed to! In an article published in *The Times Educational Supplement* of 12 November 1993, he wrote:

> So I want to say thank you – on behalf of Rudi Plaut at the Curriculum Council for Wales and myself – to all of you who have taken the trouble to write to us. What you have had to say will influence the conclusions I must reach by mid-December in order to advise the Secretary of State by the end of the year.
>
> I am not, of course, going to be able to respond in the report to the extensive analysis or range of views expressed: we need something of reasonable length! Neither am I going to be able to please everyone. But certain agreements are emerging...

Inevitably, everyone is not satisfied and the English teachers in particular feel not enough has been done to answer their concerns about assessment criteria but the Dearing Report gives hard-pressed teachers some modicum of optimism for the future. Of course, the slimming down of the curriculum, and everything which that involves, will require teachers yet again to make changes and to become familiar with yet more requirements. Most hope, however, that this will be the beginning of a different and more manageable programme.

2

TEACHERS OUT OF

CONTROL

Jill Horder

Until very recently, the word 'control' would probably have sounded rather odd to most teachers. 'Autonomy' would have been a more appropriate term to apply to the job of teaching. Post-war teachers had enjoyed an educational context of relative liberalism and economic growth, backed up by government optimism. Now, however, the context and the relationships for teaching work have changed – and they are still changing dramatically – and all the evidence indicates that this has come as a dreadful shock to many teachers. I myself was trained in 1976, an economic high-point for teachers with the implementation of the Houghton Report (DES 1974), which itself had resulted from a sustained period of government confidence in teachers and education. Now, I feel a sense of sudden cold, the apparent withdrawal of government trust in the 'professionals'; the hardly creditable threat that, having been trained in a different ideological era, I could be on the scrap heap at thirty-five!

Relationships have changed – in my opinion, for the worse. Of course there was always 'control' of teaching work: structure, authority and leadership were always needed; but the recent sea-change of public opinion against teachers has once more laid bare the basic employer–employee nexus, as the very ground shifts under teachers' feet and they are forced to reconsider their aims and purposes. In this respect it is a potentially exciting time: education has become

the site of overt political struggle. It is also a potentially de-stabiliz-
ing time as time-honoured values come under attack. Writers on the
current scene have documented euphoria or pessimism, according
to their ideological point of view. Anne Jones (1987), for example,
talks about the necessity for schools to adapt or die. She endorses
current educational initiatives and suggests ways of managing schools
that will enable them to be adaptive and responsive to change.
Others, however, document the feelings of many teachers that they
are becoming increasingly deskilled, demoralized and divided as a
profession.

Moreover, these recent changes have now, of course, been enshrined in law. Stuart Maclure (1988) documents how the Education
Reform Act of 1988, alone 'altered the basic power structure of the
education system'. Likewise, Walker and Barton (1987) detected 'a
movement of power to control and define education towards the
political centre' and 'the deliberate and determined application of
a "market ideology" as the major perceptual framework for educational planning and evaluation' which involves 'transformations in
teachers' roles and responsibilities'.

That teachers have been under attack and stripped of their former
autonomy is undeniable, given the imposition of the Teachers' Pay
and Conditions Act of 1987 which has denied teacher unions a
place in negotiating pay and conditions; and the Education Reform
Act of 1988 which imposed a National Curriculum and an entirely
new way of managing schools under local management of schools
(LMS) thus breaking up the former tripartite 'partnership' of power-
sharing by central government, local government and schools. The
new powers given to headteachers and their governing bodies, in
particular their powers to hire and fire, have changed the role of
the headteacher from that of leading professional to manager or
employer. In these circumstances, the headteacher and senior management may become increasingly divorced from the staff as the
employer–employee relationship is strengthened. In addition, teachers have felt further silenced by such developments as the abolition
of their curriculum body, the Schools Council, and the introduction of non-elected bodies such as the former Manpower Services
Commission (MSC) and more recently the School Curriculum and
Assessment Authority (SCAA).

Teachers have not only been left out of the decision-making process; they have clearly become the central target. What has been on
offer is a new concept of teachers' work or 'professionalism', externally defined and imposed. Teachers have been invited to swiftly
accept and ingest this ideological revolution or leave the profession.

The imposition of the new, wholesale, all-embracing framework

for education has been formidable for those living through it: teachers were broken as a cohesive group during the Teachers' Action of
1985–7 and, until the successful boycott of the Key Stage 3 tests during the summer of 1993, they seemed unable to challenge the new
framework in any fundamental way. In Chapter 12 of this book,
Stephen Waters provides a graphic description of the events which
led up to this boycott and the anger of teachers of English who were
expected to prepare pupils for what they saw as ill-conceived tests
which, 'jarred with and even contradicted the national curriculum
itself'. Many teachers had endorsed many of the current educational
developments such as the reform of the examination system (which
now appears to be regressing), the introduction of pupil profiling,
and the movement towards more flexible negotiated teaching and
learning styles. In this sense, the Education Reform Act of 1988 is
not revolutionary at all in that it merely imposes educational initiatives which had been thoroughly aired and discussed in previous
decades. What is new is the imposition – the determined effort by
central government to prevent teachers from having either a voice
or a power-base. It is this that has been so galling and insulting. As
the control, and more importantly, the pace of reform has been
taken out of teachers' hands, distress and frustration have resulted,
making a mockery of any true concept of 'professionalism', as teachers
have felt their own sense of effectiveness reduced.

Insofar as central government has ever framed a coherent ideology for education, this has been government's most determined
definition of education since 1944. Believing teachers and their
organizations are unable to respond fast enough to the requirements
of the modern economy in terms of providing an enterprising
workforce that can adapt swiftly to changes in the nature of work
and international competition, there has been an attempt to put
education into the market-place and to introduce mechanisms such
as parent power and the facility to 'opt out' of the existing system
in order to link education once more to what are perceived to be the
economic realities of the day and to force the profession to respond
or die.

In this context it is probably important to remember that teachers
are not the sole target of the present government – though they
may well feel so – but seem part of the wider attempt to revitalize what is regarded as an ossifying public sector, including the
National Health Service and Civil Service, by introducing, again,
the ideology of the 'market'. A similar restructuring, a similar new
language of 'efficiency', 'accountability', 'performance indicators' and
the like, are well under way. And teachers are also part of the wider
war where central government has systematically been reasserting

its right to govern against the lesser powers of local government
and trade unionism.

So successful has been the sudden shift of power to central government that every aspect of teachers' work has, it seems, been
affected and has simultaneously come under the reappraising spotlight in a dizzying flurry of change. Walker and Barton (1987) sum
up the position.

> New criteria for the content and structure of the curriculum
> have been established; new modes of assessment and of public
> examination have been evolved; new management structures
> for schools have been erected; support services have been priva-
> tised; teachers' conditions of service and salary structures have
> been redefined by dictat; the funding and resourcing of educa-
> tion has been carefully manipulated through control of award
> bodies or through the distribution of Rate and Educational
> Support Grants; a national core curriculum has been proposed;
> school accountability and teacher assessment schemes are being
> developed; vocational ideologies have come to dominate Fur-
> ther Education and the later end of secondary schooling; teacher
> training programmes have been required to conform to cen-
> trally determined criteria and principles; the list is long.

No wonder stress features so highly in recent educational literature! Walker and Barton find these changes and the pace of them
less disturbing than the government's new vision of education, as
does Ted Wragg (1988) in his brilliant exposition of the market
philosophy and its flawed logic.

The control and pace of change are also critical to teachers, wrested
as they have been from the hands of those of us who have to
implement change. The pace has been so fast that it has become,
in my view, potentially destabilizing and teachers, stripped of the
security of working within a context of trust and esteem, have felt
a reversion to the days of the Restricted Code and 'payment by
results', when teacher–state relations were strained. Gipps and Stobart (1993) quote an extract from a book by Edmond Holmes, who
was Chief Inspector for Elementary Schools in 1911. They point out
that 'some similarities are striking and much of what he writes
encapsulates the fears of teachers now'. For example:

> The teacher who is the slave of another's will cannot carry out
> his instructions except by making his pupils the slaves of his
> own will.

and

A profound distrust of the teacher was the basis of the policy of the Department.

Many writers have written recently of the deskilling effect of the recent reforms. Apple (1988) suggests that 'intensification' has been offered as a replacement for 'professionalism' and Sara Freedman (1988) diagnosed 'burnout' as the direct result of a style of management which is divorced from the interests of those it seeks to manage.

Of course, 'professionalism' was never a politically innocent concept, and was always manipulated by both the state and the teachers' unions, according to their interests. This was possible because of the historical, ambiguous class position of teachers which had made them always rather vulnerable to state control. Grace (1987) shows how there could be apparent temporary harmony between teachers and the state at certain times in their history, when it suited the state; but at a time of crisis, the state would not hesitate to lay bare the brutal fact of its ultimate overriding control. He writes:

the mechanisms of state control over organized teachers have once again become as visible and explicit as they were at the beginning of the century.

Clearly, teachers need to restore a sense of control over their own work but this can only come about if the government is willing to explore a new partnership and re-define the existing relationship with the teaching profession. As Walsh (1987) asserts:

Clearly we have already moved into a cycle of mistrust in which emphasis is laid on contractual obligations and continually enhanced rule-systems to ensure that they are met.

Bernard Barker's words still seem very relevant (1986):

Reformers have had a good run because the utopianism of the left (expecting schools to 'liberate' blacks, workers and women) and the radicalism of the right (80 per cent will be average or above) of 'Better Schools' have converged in a glorious, self-indulgent dream of scientific progress. Meanwhile, back on earth, schools have collapsed under the weight of so many great expectations.

Other authors in this book have made the point that there have been signs of a potential new partnership during the second half of 1993 as a result of Sir Ron Dearing's review of the National Curriculum and the associated arrangements for assessment, though it remains to be seen whether Dearing has any power to make any real changes to the overall framework, should they prove necessary.

Certainly most teachers believe that the government has not got the assessment system right – a crucial part of its system of educational reform, and would agree with Gipps and Stobart (1993) that,

> The national assessment system is unwieldy, judgmental, summative, high stakes and instruction-driven. What we need instead is a system in which the educational and formative purposes of assessment are paramount, and in which teachers have a key professional role . . . What we need is an education which encourages pupils to think, be creative, to reason and to cope with the challenges of the next century.

But in order to achieve education of this kind, it follows that teachers must work in an environment which allows them 'to think, be creative, to reason and to cope with the challenges of the next century'.

3

TEACHER AUTONOMY

UNDER SIEGE?

Karen Cowley

Introduction

The recent spate of government initiatives in education has not only led to a revolution in school management but has had a considerable impact on the classroom teacher. In the opinion of many teachers, the increased central control over education is a deliberate assault on the classroom teacher's autonomy and an attempt to make the education service more accountable to the taxpayer. The big question is, can accountability to the taxpayer be congruent with an individual teacher's responsibility to the taught? Is there a change in the expectations of the role of the classroom teacher? This chapter tries to establish whether increased public accountability will enhance good classroom relationships and learning or whether it is irrelevant to the core aspects of teaching.

Professional accountability

With the passing of the Education Acts of 1986 and 1988 the government has brought about fundamental changes to the way teachers and school managers are expected to be accountable to the public. Before the education reforms, teachers had considerable autonomy over their activities and over the criteria used to evaluate their work. The local education authorities (LEAs) and the then Department of Education and Science (DES) set the policy goals for schools, but these were more concerned with administrative efficiency and financial probity than with educational processes and outcomes. Some LEAs gained renown for pioneering curriculum developments or innovative curriculum strategies; others used their advisory service to promote good teaching practice and diffuse the new ideas being developed by other LEAs, institutions and organizations. Such sources greatly influenced pedagogy and curriculum in Britain but there was no compulsion for all teachers to adopt particular practices. In fact it was common for individual schools or subject departments to develop different approaches. There was never full consensus inside or outside the profession about key educational issues such as reading schemes, classroom organization, pupil groupings or pastoral care – although in specific localities or at particular times certain viewpoints prevailed more strongly than others. These issues were considered by teachers to be part of their professional realm and therefore not open to public scrutiny and judgement.

Despite the opportunities for teachers to develop individual approaches the fact remains that there was a great deal of uniformity across the nation's secondary schools. This may have been due to the natural conservatism of teachers or to the slow diffusion of ideas into the country's thousands of educational institutions. In secondary schools this conformity was often ascribed to the straitjacket effect of the examination boards. From the development of the Certificate of Secondary Education (CSE) in the late 1960s most mainstream secondary schools were preparing the majority of their students for external examination at 16-plus. In the 1980s the General Certificate of Secondary Education (GCSE) replaced the former GCE O levels and CSEs and each GCSE syllabus had to conform to national criteria in each subject area. Although these examinations were externally administered they were in fact entirely the product of the professional educational establishment. The national criteria had been developed under the aegis of the former Schools Examination Council (SEC) which was dominated by teachers, and the criteria went through a process of national consultation with the entire body of practising secondary teachers before being finalized. Examination syllabuses were developed by working groups of volunteer teachers attached to the regional examination boards. The resulting variety of approaches in content and mode of assessment reflected the diversity of professional opinion. The scrutiny and administration of GCSE examinations were taken over by the School Examinations and Assessment Council (SEAC) on which teacher influence was reduced but not eliminated, and SEAC officials continued to engage in consultation exercises with practising teachers working with the examination boards.

LEA practice did little to dispel the view that the curriculum and classroom practice were largely professional matters. At the time when the Inner London Education Authority intervened in the case of the William Tyndale School in the mid-1970s there was considerable public debate about the educational methods used at the school and the poor level of pupil achievement. Although there was much local concern about the perceived educational failures of the school there were still some public voices raised in support of the headteacher's approach. There was no universal consensus about teaching methodology and in such an ambiguous climate the principle of the teacher's professional autonomy still held sway. The unfavourable publicity from the William Tyndale case confirmed the public's belief that many schools were similarly afflicted by unwise leadership, unstructured learning and underachievement – and this led to greater insistence on central control over teachers.

In the 1980s there was increasing pressure for teachers to be more accountable to the public. The Taylor Report (DES 1977b) initiated changes in the duties undertaken by governing bodies by recommending that governors should keep under review the life and activities of schools and that headteachers should provide more information to parents about their schools.

Some LEAs started to take a closer interest in the internal processes of schools. Several encouraged their schools to use institutional self-evaluation and some, such as Oxfordshire, imposed a self-evaluation scheme in all its schools. The continuing strength of professional autonomy was demonstrated by the fact that in most areas where institutional self-evaluation was introduced the criteria were established either by teachers within the school or by educational professionals working as advisers to the LEAs. Evaluations concentrated heavily on internal school processes such as classroom and professional conduct (so reflecting most teachers' sense of responsibility to their pupils and their peers) and they provided valuable information for departmental and whole-school planning aimed at improving pupil achievement. They were mainly carried out by teachers, with rarely any input from parents or governors. The reports were often criticized for being couched in technical language and, because the process excluded non-professionals, were treated with some suspicion by those outside education. In fact, the majority of schools were not engaging in these exercises and were giving only informal accounts of their activities to governors and parents, so outside the profession there was very little objective evidence to counteract the alarming anecdotes circulating in the post-Tyndale era.

Her Majesty's Inspectorate (HMI) have traditionally been accorded a higher degree of credibility because they acted as external agents, independent of the former DES (now Department for Education) and the schools. Nevertheless HMIs were firmly part of the educational establishment. Their professional expertise and wide collective experience enabled them to make close observations of the full range of activities and achievements of the schools they visited and their resultant reports were generally considered fair by teachers. Nevertheless, HMI never published specific criteria for their judgements on the quality of schools they inspected. Neither did they take an official line; the advice was always offered as from one professional to another. It was up to LEAs or teachers to weigh up the advice they were given and adopt it if they thought it was helpful. There was never any attempt to lay down a set of rules to which all teachers had to conform. Norman Thomas (1982: 16), an ex-HMI made his views clear when he stated that 'individual divergence, if based on good evidence, is not only permissible but positively advantageous if minds are to adapt to changing circumstances'.

Professional responsibility

These examples show how professional teachers excluded outsiders from influencing the core aspects of their work. But this is not to say that teachers felt they were only responsible to themselves. A major stimulus in encouraging teachers to experiment with different teaching strategies and to develop new curricula has always been the desire to increase motivation in pupils and to raise achievement. These are the most immediate concerns of most teachers whose principal job satisfaction comes from the creative partnerships which can be forged with their pupils. Successful teachers have always been recognized as being able to spot potential in the least prepossessing individuals, to kindle interest in learning where there was none before or to capitalize on the previous experience of a child in order to promote more rapid understanding of new material. This requires a level of flexibility and degree of craft skills which can only be developed in an environment which allows a substantial measure of autonomy.

In the 1970s teachers were faced with the challenge of preparing a wider ability range of 16-plus students for public examination. They responded by piloting new curriculum developments which, by being rooted in the experiences of children, and by having schemes of assessment which included elements of coursework, greatly increased student motivation and achievement. These innovations were incorporated into the GCSE examinations and formed a major tenet of the government funded Technical and Vocational Education Initiative (TVEI). Unfortunately suspicion fell on the reliability of the GCSE results in some quarters because teachers were heavily involved in assessing their own students, despite the fact that it is part of teachers' professional work to know how to assess reliably. Moreover, the government had given SEAC powers to make sure that the examination system worked efficiently and fairly. SEAC made checks on the examination boards to ensure that all coursework marks were cross-checked by appointed moderators or by regional teacher panels. However, before schools hardly had time to introduce the new system, there were some calls for a reduction in the coursework element of GCSE examinations and consequently in the teacher's role in assessment.

Good teachers constantly use encouragement and praise to promote better learning, but they also reflect on how pupils react to different teaching strategies, classroom resources or stimuli. This interaction between the teacher and the taught has now been formalized in many of our secondary schools into the process of compiling pupil Records of Achievement. Records of Achievement were originally developed by groups of teachers as a means of giving pupils a greater sense of responsibility for their learning but the process also promotes better practice among teachers. In receiving feedback about what an individual student feels has been achieved, a teacher is in effect being appraised on the effectiveness of her or his teaching programme. Such a partnership requires a degree of mutual responsibility. Pupils trust their teachers to provide them with stimulating material at the right level and traditionally teachers have had a high degree of autonomy in the classroom in order to respond to those needs.

Teachers' sense of responsibility to the taught has informed considerable changes in professional practice and when they arrange visits out of school hours, or give generously of their time to produce school plays, and so on, they do so because they feel personal responsibility for broadening their pupils' horizons. When they spend hours fund-raising or doing DIY refurbishments in their schools they are doing so because they believe that an improved environment or better resources will increase the effectiveness of their teaching. When they give time to supervise pupils taking school dinners or doing homework after school hours they are doing so out of a sense of responsibility for the children's welfare. The extent of extracurricular activities is often seen as an indicator of a successful school

(Rutter *et al.* 1979), yet these activities invariably exist outside a teacher's contractual duties. They are a voluntary response to the perceived needs of the client group, namely the students.

Economic accountability

Since the passing of the Education Reform Act of 1988 (ERA) teachers and school managers have to account for their activities in ways determined by people other than fellow professionals. In particular the introduction of economic accountability has made schools demonstrate 'value for money in relation to the interests and concerns of those bearing the costs' (McIntyre 1989: 82), that is taxpayers, and 'to make schools more responsive to their clients – parents, pupils, the local community and employers' (Circular 7/88, para. 9 – DES 1988a). Although schools have recognized this wider clientele in the past they have done so on terms set by themselves. Now lay people have been brought into a central position in evaluating teachers' work. By making public easily quantifiable data the reforms have enabled the wider community to obtain some measures with which to compare schools, for example performance levels on centrally controlled assessments of pupils' attainment in a standardized National Curriculum. The latter has had enormous implications for the autonomy of the classroom teacher.

Most teachers have welcomed the principle of entitlement to a broad and balanced curriculum which is enshrined by the ERA. It is congruent with teachers' sense of responsibility to raise aspirations and achievement across the pupil body. However the passing of statutory orders for each National Curriculum subject has removed the substance of the classroom teacher's autonomy. This is in great contrast to the way that the SEC had previously tried to regulate the secondary school curriculum through the GCSE national criteria – by stipulating broad objectives only. This had enabled syllabuses to be modified over time as circumstances changed and also allowed the broad church of professional opinion to coexist in relative harmony, since different syllabuses could be developed to accommodate different philosophies and pedagogy. Under the National Curriculum there is only one accepted version of knowledge. This has brought into open conflict those whose opinions on the nature of knowledge differ from those in the National Curriculum Orders. Since practising teachers were deliberately under-represented on the subject working groups there was clearly little attempt to achieve compromise and consensus among those currently teaching each subject. In addition, there have been disturbing revelations in the press that the decisions of the working groups and the National

Curriculum Council have been overturned as a result of the 'pivotal role of a handful of individuals' in influencing the Secretary of State for Education (*The Times Educational Supplement*, 30 April 1993, p. 2).

Nevertheless since 1988 teachers have had to teach the National Curriculum whether or not they had reservations either in principle or in detail. Undoubtedly problems exist in some subjects where the intended progression between the levels is not apparent in practice. Teachers are in the invidious position of teaching a programme of study which they know to be educationally suspect and does not meet the needs of their pupils. The Dearing Report (Dearing 1993) acknowledged some of the difficulties teachers had had to face and offered a series of recommendations for reform, most of which were welcomed. Even so, it has become clear that in the foreseeable future teachers will no longer be proactive in developing the curriculum. They will for the most part only be able to react to whatever is handed down to them by the Secretary of State. Thus there has been a complete shift at the core of the practising teacher's working life.

It was originally thought that standardization of the curriculum would not necessarily impinge on the teacher's autonomy to decide what teaching methods to employ. However the programmes of study often include Orders which do require a specific method, for example 'organize a group enquiry' or 'hold a class discussion' It is unclear whether current shifts in approaches to teaching are the direct result of statutory requirements or whether they are an over hasty response by besieged teachers trying to cope with what Sir Ron Dearing recognized as an overloaded curriculum. In primary schools there is now more emphasis on teachers specializing in specific subjects instead of taking a more holistic view of knowledge. In those secondary schools which have had mixed ability groupings there is now more discussion on whether to set or stream pupils. Moreover, many teachers have reduced the amount of time previously spent on investigative work, unless specified in the Orders, in order to find time to cover the hundreds of statements of attainment they are required to cover.

Standardization of the curriculum has certainly reduced teacher autonomy over what is taught but on the positive side, it does ensure that each child has access to the full curriculum up to the end of Key Stage 3 (14-plus). In the past there was often such diversity in primary schools that each class could have very different experiences depending on the interest and expertise of the class teacher. Now all students will follow the same programmes of study and there will be copious documentation on the specific kinds of knowledge, skills and understanding that each child has attained at seven, 11, 14 and 16. Benjamin Bloom (1976) argued that of all the variables that affect attainment the most crucial are the previous acquired knowledge, skills and understanding which are essential for beginning a new learning task. Although it undermines teacher autonomy in several respects, the National Curriculum has provided teachers with the means to monitor progression more effectively and therefore to fulfil their personal responsibility to their pupils.

Standardization of the curriculum was an absolute prerequisite in the introduction of Standard Assessment Tests (SATS). The tests are central to the government's aim to make teachers publicly accountable for their classroom work. Assessment is an essential part of a teacher's work and, as described earlier, teachers in secondary schools were experienced in using a variety of assessment techniques as part of the GCSE. When Professor Black's Task Group on Assessment and Testing (TGAT) reported to the DES, the Report was largely welcomed by teachers because it recognized and made use of teachers' professional skills. Teachers' observations were to be used in the internal continuous assessment of pupils. TGAT recommended that some of the national external tests could be part of the normal teaching programme. The aim was to build on good classroom practice:

> A system which was not clearly linked to normal classroom assignments and which did not demand the professional skills and commitment of the teachers might be less expensive and simpler to implement but would be indefensible in that it could set in opposition the processes of learning, teaching and assessment.
>
> (TGAT 1988: para. 220)

TGAT intended the tests to provide diagnostic information for teachers and parents as well as produce data required by the government for making comparisons between schools – but the latter soon emerged as the government's main purpose for national testing. Nevertheless, despite the government's reservations on the degree of teacher involvement in the tests, the report was accepted with few amendments. However this system of assessment had been developed separately from the curriculum orders which it was designed to test. As each of these were published it became apparent that TGAT had bequeathed a bureaucratic nightmare of assessment and recording since there were hundreds of statements of attainment and dozens of attainment targets to be assessed over ten levels. This produced major organizational difficulties for schools and interfered with, rather than complemented the teaching and learning of the curriculum. When protests were raised, the Secretary of State's response was to call for more short 'pencil and paper tests' – i.e. much simpler and easier to mark but not part of the normal teaching and learning process and inappropriate for diagnosing weaknesses in learning.

This has posed a moral dilemma for teachers. They want their pupils to be able to show what they understand and can do. They know that most learners do this most successfully in familiar surroundings, doing work which is a normal part of school life. To provide tests on the lines envisaged by the Secretary of State for every child, for every subject on the curriculum and for every attainment target in the National Curriculum has led to a massive workload for teachers. Teachers want the diagnostic information that good tests might provide but they have become frustrated when some of the lessons of the pilot tests have not been heeded. The curriculum is in turmoil with some subject orders being rewritten after students have embarked on the course. The growing disquiet and indignation of teachers about the testing arrangements in 1993 was not only about teacher workload but also because teachers felt they were failing in their responsibility to their students by putting them through unsound tests which, in some cases, were detached from the curriculum they had been following.

There seem to be no end to the demands for accountability. For example, all teachers are now to be appraised by colleagues in their own schools in order to assist them in their professional development and to identify ways of improving their skills and performance (DFE 1991, para. 4). In addition, each school is to be inspected every four years by a team appointed by the Office for Standards in Education (OFSTED) which includes lay people in its inspection teams. A summary of each inspection report will be made public and the purpose is to improve the quality of schools by providing information which will enable schools' performance to be compared by parents and the government and to monitor financial efficiency (Education Schools Act of 1992).

Does accountability raise standards?

The creation of such a variety of methods to make teachers more publicly accountable is a clear message that the government believes that professional accountability had been found wanting as a way of raising standards in schools. Instead, the Education Reform Acts of 1986 and 1988 have encouraged competition among schools. Publicized test results and inspections, including audits on financial efficiency, are the indicators being used to provide the basis of this comparison. Paradoxically, schools have less control over these kinds of performance indicators than over their own internal processes.

Headteachers have always had the power to manage and direct resources within their schools through staff deployment and the allocation of capitation funds, but local management of schools (LMS) has simply made money the unit of account in the internal management of schools – and money is allocated to each school according to the number of pupils it can attract. In fact formula funding is not fair to all schools. Some catchment areas may have declining populations; some schools have much higher running costs historically than others. The claim that market forces reward successful schools is refuted by the many reported cases of popular schools being oversubscribed and yet needing to make staff redundant in order to make the books balance.

Secondary teachers have always been responsible and accountable for the examination results achieved by their students – but the difference is that they are now widely available for comparison. This was more acceptable when teachers had full control over determining the curriculum and the methods of assessment. Now teachers have little control over these core aspects of teaching. They continue to work within an environment in which many external factors influence the quality of pupil achievement, such as the character of the schools' catchment areas and the measured ability of the pupils who enter the school. This kind of competition seems both unfair and unreal and most teachers find it hard to understand how it can raise standards.

On the other hand, much less emphasis is being placed on schools' internal processes, which research has shown do correlate closely with higher pupil achievement, such as the school's ethos (Rutter *et al.* 1979) and the effectiveness of school organization and teacher quality (Smith and Tomlinson 1989).

Many features introduced into schools under the umbrella of economic accountability appear to be completely unrelated to the core aspects of teaching which influence pupil motivation and attainment. Instead of enhancing good classroom relationships and learning by increasing the professional skills of teachers the reforms have resulted in the deskilling of teachers and the denigration of their professional competence.

Researchers have found the quest to determine the factors leading to an effective school elusive, but all would agree that a successful school has well-motivated teachers whose sense of personal responsibility to their pupils consistently results in high expectations and achievement. As the Education Reform Act bureaucracy engulfs everything in paperwork many of the features of school life which foster such a climate of high achievement may go by the board. Undoubtedly professional autonomy was not a sufficient way of achieving public accountability. Nevertheless, a form of accountability which starts by totally undermining teacher autonomy is positively damaging.

A better balance must be achieved between professional and economic accountability. In return for regaining a greater measure of autonomy over the core aspect of teaching, teachers must now expect to be evaluated against externally imposed criteria. Personal responsibility towards pupils cannot be ensured through legislation, but it is a key factor at all levels of an organization if that organization is to be responsive and effective. As we approach the year 2000 that should be the goal of every educational institution which is wishing to prepare young people to take a full and active role in society.

Part two

TEACHERS' CAREERS

4

NEW TO TEACHING

Rosemary Chapman

Never having been particularly interested in children, it was a revelation to me how much pleasure I found in their company after I had had my own. Throughout their school life, I had conscientiously attended parents' evenings, talked to staff about my children's progress, and spent some time in the classroom as a volunteer parent helper. Over a period of time, I began to think I might like to teach when my children were older and so, when my youngest child reached 3 and I reached 34, I went, just for an informal chat, to the local Careers Advice Centre. Six months later I began a one-year maths General Certificate of Secondary Education (GCSE) course at night school, followed by a year's Access course in English Language and Literature, designed to prepare adults for admission to higher education. I told myself that I was now a very different person from the girl who had little interest in learning at the age of 16. Since my school days, I had worked as a secretary for 10 years, got married and had five children and surely would have the self-confidence borne of maturity to enjoy education the second time round. However, I was dismayed to find that when faced with a large group of people my emotions had not changed much since I was 16. My hoped for self-assurance failed to realize itself at a very early stage. I still remember the first English discussion group when members of the group seemed immediately to understand that the poet MacBeth's poem 'Scissors' contained allegorical references to homosexuality. First, I was unsure what 'allegorical' meant and secondly, the description of a drawer full of cutlery seemed an awful long way from society's response to the gay community! It took me 40 minutes to speak and that was only after rehearsing my statement three times in my head. My heart was pounding waiting for a space in the proceedings into which to stab my sentence. I recalled vividly Mr Hill, my old A Level History teacher saying, 'You've gone the same colour as your jumper, Rosemary' (our uniform was maroon). Apart from being two stones heavier and more tired, I could easily have been sitting in Mr Hill's class.

Gradually, I came to understand that we were not expected to possess a certain quotient of knowledge or have a variety of skills before entering the course. Staff were very supportive and we were encouraged to express our views. We were spoon-fed a great deal during the first six sessions, and I was grateful for that. From then on, I decided that I had heard far more wild offerings that the ones I proposed to voice, and so found it much easier to participate.

The workload on the two-morning-a-week Access course was heavy. In fact, it proved to be more demanding than the actual BEd course as it consisted of reading one book every three sessions, discussing it in class and producing one essay of 2000 to 2500 words each week on various aspects of the text, together with a weekly language homework. Not everyone stayed the course. I suspected then, and still do now, that this was to 'weed out' those who might find the degree course overpowering.

I managed to pass GCSE maths, did well on the Access course and then applied for and was accepted on a four-year BEd course. I should have felt confident at jumping these two hurdles, but my overwhelming feeling was one of relief that my shortcomings had never been detected by my lecturers. I have to admit occasionally even now to the same emotions with regard to both parents and teachers at the school in which I teach. Perhaps it takes a long time for mature students to feel totally confident in an environment in which we may have previously felt something of a failure.

Over half the students on the BEd course were 'mature', if not as mature as I was. I did not have an auspicious start. At times, I found the lectures impossible to follow and blamed myself for attempting the course while trying to juggle family and personal commitments to suit myself. Half my own group failed the first assignment while I just achieved half a mark over the pass/fail divide. The results of this first assignment had a marked effect on my self-esteem until I discovered that other groups taught by other lecturers had very different results. I began to question the likelihood of one group performing so disastrously when others had achieved good results. What struck me forcibly during my initial training was the old chestnut from my schooldays – that it is the respect and liking students have for their teacher that determines the extent to which students understand or want to learn.

If all lecturers were excellent, it might be supposed that all BEd students would emerge as enthusiastic, well-informed teachers-to-be, with a folder full of new if as yet untried ideas for each curriculum area. Knowledge of human nature should have told me that this was unlikely to happen. As the course went on, I discovered that lecturers' ability to communicate with students varied, and that this first unnerving experience was not typical of the course as a whole. I began to appraise college lecturers and to appreciate that even the best would be unlikely to maintain a 100 per cent record of excellence throughout the whole of their academic career.

Looking back, I see that this early near-failure and the following discussions with staff, led me to have the confidence to admit at an early stage what I did not understand and to consider ways in which not only to improve my ability to understand, but also to suggest to lecturers ways in which information might be presented in a more digestible format. I found they almost always responded positively and problems were generally ironed out quickly. Perhaps my age did help in this respect because I was often elected as a 'non-aggressive' spokesperson for the group on the rare occasions when we wanted to raise seemingly intractable problems. On the whole, I came to appreciate that lecturers did their best for us over the four years. I put a great deal of effort into reading, researching, note-taking *and* listening, and I reached the stage when I rarely felt my lack of understanding was the result of lack of ability.

Teaching practice

Teaching practice was an exhausting experience. It was daunting to take a class with the class teacher, headteacher or tutor making notes on progress. As the basic lecturing was split into three areas, academically quite separate from each other (teaching practice, degree level English and curriculum studies spanning the whole curriculum), there were perhaps inevitably gaps for which no lecturers were prepared to take responsibility. No tutors seemed to think it was within their jurisdiction to provide us with guidance about classroom discipline, well known as the newly qualified teacher's biggest headache. This was left to the class teacher. The teaching practice tutor generally mentioned this important issue only when we had been marked down for dealing inadequately with a problem.

I think we all felt that we needed time to observe the ways teachers
dealt with discipline and organization in action in a variety of classroom environments and with a variety of age groups. It would have
been useful to ask class teachers quite openly which approaches
they used and why, without having to pretend we were in posses-
sion of all the necessary know-how – and without fear of being
marked down for demonstrating an inability to cope.

Lecturers tended to tell us what to teach and sometimes how to
teach it *in principle*, but rarely referred to the specifics of how to
teach exciting ideas such as tie-dye, clay modelling and technology, to a class of 30 infant children with no adult help! Students
can inform themselves about different approaches by drawing on
relevant literature, studying the National Curriculum and other
guidelines, but nothing beats the experience of someone who is able
to report personal experience, discuss the likely pitfalls of working
in an actual classroom, and who can draw on examples of alternative
approaches. Better to be able to take advantage of someone else's
experience in a non-threatening environment, than make mistakes
on the public platform of the classroom during teaching practice.

Now, I am reminded of the importance of positive discipline every
day in my own classroom. If I cannot manage a class sufficiently
well, the most invigorating and original lessons will fail. If I cannot
control children using positive means wherever possible, then their
self-esteem and motivation will be damaged.

Throughout the whole 21-week period of teaching practice, I was
continually overwhelmed with the sheer weight of paperwork and
what I firmly believe to be too-detailed preparation for every lesson.
With each lesson plan had to come aims and objectives; introduction; central theme and future intentions, all tied in with attainment
targets and schemes of work for each subject. Evaluations were required for each lesson, describing positive or negative experiences
and plans for the future development and daily progress of each
child.

It seemed inconceivable that practising teachers would ever have
the time for so much detailed preparation, and that has proved to
be the case. Official records in my school are completed half-termly
and ongoing records are kept up to date, but certainly not on a
daily basis for each child. There seems little justification for teaching practice bearing so little relation to the real world and I cannot
understand why more realistic methods of preparing for classes
cannot be devised.

Because of this overwhelming workload, I always found that no
matter how well meaning, supportive and well organized a school
was – and most of them were – teaching practice was always some-

thing to be endured and overcome. Only now that I have begun 'real' teaching have I really enjoyed children's company in the classroom, found time to stand back and assess their progress and their relationships with peers and to try out adventurous activities which might or might not succeed. The opportunity to take risks in order to try out new ideas is now one of my greatest pleasures.

Although many of my comments about the organization of the BEd and teaching practice tend to be critical, the course itself made me confident in my ability to pass formal examinations, formulate assignments on a variety of topics, and locate information from a variety of sources. It gave me the expertise and enthusiasm to give of my best to the children I teach. My own family was inordinately proud when I received a First Class pass, especially when they knew I had previously taken maths O Level three times at school and failed every time, and had gained only mediocre passes at O Level.

Applying for a job

We had very little guidance from college about interview techniques or the filling in of application forms. Perhaps the lecturers felt we should be able to cope with all that, and perhaps they were right, but I found I had to learn the hard way. Obtaining a teaching post was certainly not plain sailing. Rejection slips from 10 schools to which I first applied led me to look again at the way I completed forms and letters of application. I decided I had to take far more care about directing the application to the specific requirements of the particular school and eventually, I was called for interview. Four failures and subsequent debriefings led me to develop a more successful interview persona. On my final teaching practice, the BEd co-ordinator had placed me at the closest school possible to my own home. It was a friendly and supportive establishment to children, students, teachers and parents, and I learned more there than in any other school. I was eventually fortunate enough to be offered a temporary post to cover for a teacher on maternity leave, and to have responsibility for the class I had taught on teaching practice.

Starting work as a newly qualified teacher

I am fortunate to be working in a school I like, albeit in a temporary post, and with colleagues who are very supportive. In 'real' teaching, I find I am learning something new every day, from the best consistency of paint to use on plastic pots, to the most successful ways of dealing with individual behavioural problems. It is like passing a driving test. When you have passed, you think you know how to drive, only to realize how much more you really need to learn.

Teaching to the National Curriculum has caused few problems. I have not had to adapt my approach to conform to the requirements of the National Curriculum as has been the case for experienced colleagues, because I have known nothing else. It has been there since my first year in college and my first year of teaching. It has provided me with a supportive framework within which to work. I have not felt overloaded by the curriculum, but as my children are four and five year-olds, my experience must be very different from that of teachers of more senior classes. They are having to cope with complex procedures and tend to have a much more prescriptive timetable. As I become more experienced, I may come to resent what my colleagues see as unacceptable government control of the curriculum, but I have no past as a teacher and so I do not see my professionalism as being challenged.

How much time I would have to spend with other adults in the classroom never really occurred to me while in college. I was accustomed to being observed during teaching practice, but parents, nursery nurses, classroom assistants, advisory teachers and students, all share my classroom. As a mature teacher, I am accustomed to forming relationships with fellow parents, and creating positive relationships with people in the classroom has not presented any difficulties. Possibly I have an advantage over the newly qualified 21 and 22 year-olds, but I welcome the presence of other adults and we work well together.

It came as a surprise to realize that parents could feel nervous at times when speaking to or working with a teacher, and even more surprising was the discovery that all teachers felt nervous on the first day of term and on the day of parent–teacher meetings. As a parent, it never occurred to me that my children's teacher could possibly be anything but relaxed during an interview with me.

What has proved to be a continuing burden is the keeping of official reports. Each record of a child's progress takes up to an hour to complete, and preliminary observations take much longer. Teachers who are to receive the children in the next school year are daunted by the sheer bulk of the documentation and despairingly ask for 'just a paragraph about what the children are really like, and where they are on the schemes so we can see at a glance'. This request is not made out of laziness, but out of a desire to see a succinct, to-the-point précis of a child's progress. I think we all feel that somehow or another something will have to be done to reduce the amount of paperwork to a level which is of maximum help to the children *and* their teachers.

Gradually, I have come to understand the weight of responsibility which headteachers and teachers have had to shoulder since the full impact of the government's education reforms have been felt in schools. I realize why so many teachers are weary at the amount of information, rules and new Orders, which in some cases have involved a total rethink of principles and practices. Experienced teachers have felt their values to be threatened and it is easy to see why. Perhaps all this change will be good for the profession in the long run, but until the pace of change eases and the paperwork and required documentation are reduced, teaching is going to be hard.

I am still learning and am grateful for the encouragement and support of my experienced colleagues. I have committed six years of my life to preparing to teach and in the process have accumulated a sizeable student loan which will have to be paid off from my earnings. I enjoy what I am doing but I find the work exacting. Every day is a challenge and no-one who has not taught can possibly understand the exhaustion I feel at the end of a working day. Even so, I have never enjoyed a job so much. I feel I am becoming more confident all the time. I like the children and I like my colleagues. All I need now is a permanent post – and the strength to face the next 20 years.

5

IN MID-CAREER

Andrew Spencer

As an English teacher in mid-career, I am feeling like Macbeth. In these turbulent times I am 'not without ambition' but 'I have no spur to prick the sides of my intent' – so this chapter represents a personal search for the causes of my career inertia at the age of 39. In particular, I want to test a common belief among teachers that the current climate of change has had a deleterious effect upon some careers, and, I want to examine the prospects for the second half of my working life by identifying some coping strategies.

The approach I have taken is to present an autobiographical picture of my career, connecting this to mediating influences of change. Although idiosyncratic, this autobiographical approach may strike a chord with other teachers and fuel further discussion about the extent to which change has affected both the objective and subjective careers of teachers.

Research into teachers' lives and careers suggests that I should not be surprised at my condition. Several works have identified anything between five and eight stages, phases or themes experienced by teachers during their working lives (Sikes *et al.* 1985; Hargreaves and Fullan 1992; Maclean 1992; Huberman 1993). Two of these studies identify themes of crisis and uncertainty in mid-career after 15 to 20 years' service. Coinciding with Jung's (1926) 'dangerous period', this phase is characterized by a coming to terms with, and, adapting to a career plateau, self-reappraisal and questioning (Sikes *et al.* 1985), disenchantment, the drawing up of a balance sheet of personal and professional achievement and envisaging the future (Huberman 1993). These observations pose a conundrum. Is this mid-career phenomenon 'wired in some way into the psychological evolution of the teacher' (Huberman 1993), or is it induced, or, exacerbated by personal, institutional and external determinants? By isolating the perceived effects of educational change upon my own career, I may begin to understand the extent of its influence over and above other factors.

A multi-dimensional concept of career underpins the following analysis. These dimensions emerge from a broader interpretation of Hughes' (1937) well-known objective and subjective career classifi- cations. The objective meaning of career conveys a sequence of movements within a structured occupational hierarchy. It is syn- onymous, although not exclusively so, with advancement, progres- sion and ascendancy. Of course, higher status, more responsibility and salary enhancements are not necessarily the primary career goals of all teachers but this dimension is relevant to the task of assessing the extent to which educational change expedites or impedes careerism. Two strands are discernible within a subjective interpre- tation of career. In this domain, career may be viewed as 'a sort of running adjustment between a man [sic] and the various facts of life and of his [sic] professional world' (Hughes 1958). It also speaks of commitment and recognizes the possibility that this may vary not just across the teaching force but also during an individual's work- ing life. The combined effect of this broader conception of career is to suggest that adjustments and their triggers, variations to levels of commitment and their causes, are just as much the constituents of a career profile as the factors which enhance or inhibit promotion. It also reflects the holistic view that life outside school impacts upon career and that the latter is influenced by the history of each indi- vidual's time.

Origins and early career

I recall being intent upon a career in teaching from an early age. My own teachers influenced an impressionable mind. These people were gods, imparting their wisdom and wit, holding us spellbound with readings from literary tales and motivating us towards sporting prowess. High status members of the local community, simultane- ously instructors and judges, there was something noble, theatrical, solid and secure about their presence and practice. My play imitated them and I remember my parents' encouragement when I articulated my desire to teach. At grammar school, targets were clear: O Levels and A Levels then a teacher training establishment. Prefectorial minding of younger pupils' study periods and managership of a lower school sports team, gave me a foretaste of teacher–pupil relationships before embarking upon three years training. In attempting to identify the appeal of teaching to me as a youngster in the 1960s, three features emerge from this reflection. Could it have been the status of the role within and beyond its people-changing relationship that seemed attractive?

With the secondary sector in the forefront of my experience, this was the age range I aspired towards but a most remarkable feature of my career origins was the decision about which subject to specialize in. At interview with the college principal, it emerged that my headteacher had alluded to some theatrical talent in his reference and I was persuaded to study drama. The realization now that subject status can influence both the objective and subjective careers of teachers (Bennett 1985) raises significant issues about subject selection for initial training. Expressed in its simplest terms, research suggests that those intent upon promotion would do well to specialize in high status core subjects. Some dimensions of career can therefore be a spoil or a casualty of the connections between subject expertise and subject status. My choice, born solely out of perceived subject expertise, would prove in time to be both fortuitous and an impediment to my career development.

After acquiring subject knowledge, learning about theories of education and gaining initial practical experience during the three years of training, I secured my first post in September 1975 as the drama specialist in a large, mixed secondary modern school. I felt confident about applying my knowledge and expertise, and my career debut coincided with the pay award granted as a result of the Houghton Report (DES 1974) which temporarily restored parity with similar occupations. I recall nothing but positive feelings during my probationary year. Job security, a good rate of guaranteed remuneration, specialist drama facilities equal to those enjoyed during initial training and sole responsibility for the subject, gave scope for development and the freedom to be creative which stimulated a high level of commitment. I enjoyed a free rein, felt trusted as a competent professional and could devise my own schemes of work for the subject. With no domestic ties, much of my social life revolved around activities with school colleagues. Trips to the theatre were organized and as a young teacher I was quickly absorbed into the sporting life of the school, spending one evening a week coaching one of the football teams for Saturday morning fixtures. Annual school holidays to locations at home and abroad were experienced and during the first five years of my career I taught English to Spanish pupils at a Jesuit college in Las Palmas during the summer vacation.

Two years into my career, the school changed its character and became a comprehensive establishment. This change required all the teachers to reapply for their positions and as a result I was awarded a Scale 2 post as teacher-in-charge of drama. During the mid-1970s, many experienced teachers had secured secondment to read for a BEd degree. It was a rolling response to the James Report's (DES 1972) recommendation that teaching should become an all graduate profession. Understandably, faced with an influx of young graduates, teachers without degrees wanted to protect their status but it was also an opportunity to earn extra salary increments. Caught up in the dash for qualifications, I enrolled for an ADB(Ed) advanced drama in education qualification, tutored by the local education authority's (LEA's) drama adviser. This not only equipped me with more knowledge and broadened my repertoire of teaching skills but also put me under the authority's spotlight.

Looking back, these too were times of change. My subject was making inroads into the school curriculum as a result of its experiential, discovery-learning qualities, heralded by the prominent and influential work of Dorothy Heathcote. The Schools Council published a report extolling the virtues of drama in education and one of the General Certificate of Education (GCE) examining boards launched new O Level syllabuses in drama and theatre arts. I wanted to be in the vanguard of these developments and with the encouragement of my headteacher, we adopted the O Level course and pioneered it within the authority. This led to my being appointed a visiting examiner for the subject and as other schools developed the courses, I was invited to lecture at LEA in-service courses.

These were the late 1970s and by now the Great Debate had stimulated a national 11–16 Curriculum Inquiry. My school, recognized as an efficient and innovative one within the authority, was invited to participate in the study. This involvement lasted for a number of years and encouraged us to rethink the delivery of our curriculum. We were asked to substitute the traditional model of aims, objectives and content with a new approach concentrating on knowledge, skills, attitudes and cross-curricular input into areas of experience. Along with my colleagues, I designed and implemented projects, wrote working papers about them and held discussions with Her Majesty's Inspectorate (HMI).

We were in the forefront of experimentation and this close participation enkindled a highly satisfying, purposeful and professional atmosphere. Out of the blue I was promoted for a second time and an assistant drama teacher was appointed to the school. Having established myself in the post, I still felt at a disadvantage without graduate status so for professional development and as a personal challenge, I commenced study for an Open University degree in the arts and education. I was 25, on a Scale 3, still free from any domestic responsibilities and very happy in my work.

This beginning phase in my career displays many of the classic characteristics outlined in the research: experimentation, stabilization and definite commitment. Change had a positive influence upon both dimensions of my career. Comprehensivization brought promotion; national developments, raising the status of my subject, led to personal recognition within the organized community; involvement in the Great Debate's curriculum reform initiative heightened our sense of partnership and professionalism and the shift towards an all graduate teaching force acted as a spur to increase personal knowledge and expertise. These changes encouraged my colleagues and me to reflect upon and modify our curriculum designs. At that time they were our schemes but I think we accepted the need to update them and did not foresee a serious challenge to teacher ownership of the content and methodology of the curriculum. Subjectively, school and life seemed in harmony. I was part of a group of young, enterprising teachers, managed by a very experienced and innovative headteacher.

By the early 1980s I faced a career dilemma. I had secured rapid promotion and realized that I had reached a plateau. Drama was still enjoying high profile nationally but advertisements in the educational press suggested to me that its teachers stood little chance of progressing beyond the point I had reached in the pay structure. Either I would have to accept the subject's low status and its career implication or diversify in order to advance objectively. Loyalty to the subject was therefore challenged but fortunately drama traditionally has close ties with English and a supportive headteacher facilitated the opportunity to teach English and English Literature to GCE level in addition to continuing my departmental responsibilities for drama. English is a high status subject and I felt that I had succeeded in negotiating my way out of possible career stagnation.

After building on a couple of years' experience of English teaching I was appointed to a Scale 4 head of English and drama post in a semi-rural Roman Catholic comprehensive school within the same authority. The diversification had paid dividends and the move occurred when I was in the early stages of studying for an advanced diploma in educational management. At that time, new arrangements for the national funding of INSET (Inservice Education of Teachers) had prioritized management as a core skill for development in education and I espied the currency value of the qualification as an investment for further career advancement. I think the move acted as a fillip to commitment as a new and challenging era began, and, as a practising Roman Catholic, I felt a more complete teacher in this environment as traditionally Catholic education makes no distinction between secular and religious content within the whole curriculum.

During the first five years in post, relationships were built with colleagues and pupils, the department strengthened its resources and developed its syllabus effectively and consistently achieved good examination results. Once again I found myself involved with school activities abroad and I directed some school productions. I had begun to tutor in educational management for the Open University and had made my first venture into authorship (Spencer 1989). I was also co-opted onto my local primary school's governing body and served as vice-chair and acting-chair for a time. I attended a residential course on the role of the secondary deputy and felt that the time was right to apply for deputy headships.

Mid-career

My career story to this stage would appear to be about experiences driven by and influencing the pursuit of advancement in the occupational hierarchy of teaching. Only one main adjustment occurred which was to achieve subject diversification with support from the headteacher. High levels of commitment seem to have been sustained except for a dip when a career plateau had been reached. With no competing demands outside work, my career was at its peak of energy, involvement, ambition and self-confidence.

Now, in mid-career, I feel different. Whereas previously I seemed able to progress to a timetable, now that progress is less certain and although the desire for it remains, it is cooler. I am experiencing a phase of career reassessment because I know I should have been a deputy headteacher by now. Interviews went well but de-briefings always revealed the lack of a specific skill. A lack of pastoral management experience was remedied when the headteacher offered me a head of year role to broaden my experience, but then came the reforms. Many teachers felt that the General Certificate of Secondary Education (GCSE) had been introduced with undue haste but we absorbed it. Then the National Curriculum statutory Orders for English (which specified curriculum content and assessment procedures) were issued and their interpretation was cascaded to colleagues. Concurrently, my school was a member of a local Technical and Vocational Education Initiative (TVEI) consortium and needed to implement Records of Achievement. Local management of schools (LMS) heralded the appearance of computer-aided administration and the training of staff to manage it. Further strands within the National Curriculum meant that cross-curricular themes and issues had to be developed, and assessment, recording and reporting became an important feature. The LEA scheme for teacher appraisal needed to be assimilated into the school's approach to staff development. The spectre of OFSTED inspection was materializing and changes in the delivery of initial teacher training was bringing more responsibility for it to schools. These waves of change have washed over my experience during the past five years but somehow, unlike the changes occurring in the early stage of my career, I have not ridden them and turned them to my advantage. I believe that development of expertise in some of these topics of change would have invigorated my career but I seek now an explanation for why this has not happened.

An opening observation is that my experiences in preparation for deputy headship lagged behind those required for its modern role and the sheer pace of change meant I was always playing catch-up. The school was a small one, on the southern boundary of a large LEA and therefore out on a limb. When changes were being implemented in my first school, we were closer to the external agents of change and had recourse to their advice. School size may also be a factor determining the degree of influence change can have on career. My contention is that embracing some management responsibility for some of the changes may have added impetus to a flagging career but in a small school, headteachers may feel more inclined to reserve control of externally imposed initiatives for the senior management domain. Some may also assume that their middle managers, who may already be combining more than one role, cannot accept more responsibility. The third scenario is that some headteachers may have used change as an opportunity to promote former Scale 2 teachers who lost status when the new incentive allowances scheme was introduced in the mid-1980s.

Another feature of the changes during the era of reform was that they targeted the organizational infrastructures of schools and crossed the traditional subject boundaries. Perhaps as a consequence there has been a proliferation in the number of co-ordinator roles, usually, for the reason stated above, adopted by teachers below head of department or faculty level. Although some schools have appointed a teacher-in-charge of computer-aided administration, others have taken the view, in the interests of stability, continuity and freeing the teachers to teach, that it would be better for clerical staff under the supervision of a bursar, to accommodate this change.

Whereas some schools have managed the reforms under these constraints and by these strategies, others have not. These factors and the managerial approaches to change just outlined, form the restricted context of my experience at a crucial time in my career. As an ambitious head of department, I faced an increasing workload involving the production of new schemes of work for Key Stages 3 and 4 of the National Curriculum, implementing new arrangements for the assessment and testing of pupils, and budgeting for the delivery of the English curriculum. I suggest it is because of subject overload that the roles and opportunities which traditionally and contemporaneously could be acquired for career advancement by aspiring deputy heads, are going instead to capable colleagues who are placed lower in the structural hierarchy.

The response to this re-assessment of my career was a realization that I needed to work in a school where some of these career-building experiences could be gained. I therefore faced a second critical moment of re-adjustment in my career and effected a lateral move (in terms of pay) by securing the post of Head of Humanities in a larger school which affords opportunities to participate in management of the changes. This represents a tactical withdrawal from the interview circuit to acquire relevant experience but having executed this move, why are my feelings dominated by a disturbing sense of indifference towards my work? Perhaps it is because the previously unilinear focus on career as ascending the hierarchy has widened with age and experience. A desire 'to establish a niche in society' (Levinson et al. 1978) led recently to my being commissioned as a Justice of the Peace which brings a new perspective to my life. Family bereavement too has undoubtedly altered that life and pre-occupied my mind for some considerable time. Less than full ideological commitment to some of the features of the National Curriculum also accounts for some of the indifference.

The future

What begins to emerge from this personal reassessment of my work experience is that there is an ambivalent relationship between change and career. In the objective domain, involvement in the management of change can promote career advancement but in its subjective sense, a career can suffer a decrease in commitment if there is too much change or the change is unpopular. The plethora of change in educational policy brings mixed fortunes to teachers in mid-career. Ambitious teachers who have the opportunity to manage the implementation of change may derive career benefits from this but in my own experiences, two factors intervene in this process. First, even though the inclination towards involvement may be strong, the opportunity to participate may favour teachers on structural levels below that occupied by an aspiring deputy head. Secondly, and more obviously, participation in the management of whole-school change is at the discretion of the headteacher, whose decisions in turn may be constrained by the geographical location and size of the school, in deciding priorities and personnel to lead the implementation of change.

If such opportunities are denied, if personal commitment is threatened by ideological opposition to change or if the phenomenon of mid-career crisis strikes, what coping strategies can teachers fall back on to revitalize their careers for the second half of their working lives?

1 It is ironic that as teachers, we stress the importance of self-reflection to our pupils but that our own adult exchanges about working life tend to be superficial and fragmentary. More profound, professional reflection can be enriching and empowering. Through staff development and appraisal schemes, structures exist in schools to facilitate the oral equivalent of this chapter's exercise but in mid-career and beyond, appraisees might welcome a more cathartic experience leading towards meeting the needs of the whole person rather than just the teacher person.

2 Although headteachers have the right to retain or delegate managerial responsibility for the implementation of change, teachers looking to secure involvement would be well advised to 'read the organization' (Lyons and McCleary 1980), anticipate developments and be assertive in pursuing participation.

3 If, as in my own case, opportunities for involvement in the implementation of change at managerial level are denied, tactical withdrawal can be considered as opposed to the more counter-productive 'psychological withdrawal' (Sikes *et al.* 1985). This usually involves a horizontal career move to an environment that can offer the kind of experience required.

4 The collapse of the ill-fated Standard Assessment Tests (SATs) in 1993, highlighted the depth of opposition by teachers to one feature of the recent reforms. The SATs were a seasonal feature of the National Curriculum but teachers may also feel opposed to some aspects of the day-to-day delivery of subject programmes of study which in turn leads to a lessening of career commitment. It has been suggested that in these circumstances some teachers engage in 'positive focusing' (Huberman 1993) by adapting curriculum packages and claiming ownership of them. Teachers affected in this way, by imposition, could be encouraged to see

how closely their current practice reflects statutory programmes of study.

5 To compensate for career inertia or mid-career crisis, concurrent or parallel careers to teaching could be pursued. Teachers continue to play important community roles and these may be viewed as the value-added dimensions which can enrich the quality of teaching. Concurrent career roles are not signs of career disenchantment, failure or a lessening of commitment but a recognition that teachers can and should play wider roles in the community because of the particular knowledge, expertise and perspectives they can offer.

It has been surmised that 'future books on the teaching career might record ... how much things have changed' (Haigh 1993). Teachers in mid-career during the era of reform will testify to that, while registering a degree of metaphorical affinity with John's 'people who have been through the great persecution' (Revelations 7:14). It is a tract for our times but perhaps more life history studies of teachers' careers will herald a 'gentler, post-modern sort of time' (Haigh 1993).

6

FROM MIDDLE TO

SENIOR MANAGEMENT

John Ross

The backcloth of educational change

The British Education service is undergoing its most radical period of change since the 1944 Education Act. The National Curriculum, its associated assessment and testing, local management of schools, the establishment of grant maintained schools and City Technology Colleges: these are among the many factors altering the educational landscape in a manner unimaginable 10 years ago.

By requiring schools to operate within the framework of locally devolved budgets, management tasks, management styles and structures and the roles undertaken within them have changed. Recent Education Acts can be perceived as an attempt to alter the culture of schools, which are increasingly involved with development plans, and are places where organizational objectives are evaluated, developed and reviewed. This makes the role of the senior manager demanding and exacting, yet also exciting and fulfilling.

Middle management experience: working under pressure

My previous post was as director of music in a church aided inner-city comprehensive, where I remained for nearly eight years. It was and still is a good school to work in. Pupils were talented and enthusiastic, and parents, governors, and the headteacher readily gave their support. As musical standards rose, so did the frequency of public performances. In my last 18 months at the school these included performing in five cathedrals and two concert tours abroad. The high standard of performance attained by so many students was the icing on the cake in a very rewarding yet also very demanding post.

Communication could be difficult. Major concerts and services involved over 100 performers, frequently including former students who would return for these events. Internal communications within the school depended somewhat precariously on a daily bulletin inserted into every register. As lunch was staggered it was impossible to bring all performers together during the working day. My own lunch was often a sandwich hastily snatched between two rehearsals which were in turn squeezed between two lessons, a situation all too familiar to many music teachers.

I had a superbly resourced department, although it was spread over three floors. As I was the focal point of the department, all matters were channelled through me, from the trivia of unlocking doors to the responsibility for arranging travel, suitable accommodation for 115 people, and concert venues in the Strasbourg region.

A substantial component of the music curriculum was taught by visiting specialists, which gave all pupils hands-on experience of a wide range of musical styles. This was excellent in theory, but my own teaching became susceptible to interruptions; not infrequently I would have to abandon my lesson to investigate why a class was without a visiting teacher two floors below.

The paradox was that the more busy and successful the department became, the greater were the pressures to keep it afloat. A major problem was the lack of people to whom I could delegate, as the department had few full-time staff. Having gained a reputation for good music we could not afford to put on an indifferent concert, or postpone an event because it had been impossible to get everyone together for a key rehearsal. Holidays merged into term times, as they were taken up with rehearsals or performances, or were used to catch up on the pile of paperwork which had built up.

Teaching and institutional stress

What makes teaching so stressful and exhausting is not so much the actual teaching, demanding though that is. Nor is it the leading of clubs, societies, coaching sports teams, directing music or drama rehearsals: we offer these because they are our strengths and we mostly enjoy them. What makes the profession so demanding is the burden of administration and paperwork required, coupled with frequent criticism in the media by politicians and other interest groups. Heads in schools struggle to lift the morale of colleagues, but they are being thwarted by weekly pronouncements on falling standards in the classroom, truancy figures, examination league tables, the failure of schools to teach the difference between right and wrong, and so on.

This constant criticism can result in what Freedman (1988) describes as the phenomenon of teacher 'burnout' – a manifestation of anger and frustration, particularly in young teachers whose career options are still open. Freedman's analysis explains this 'burnout' as arising not from the overtaxing of intellectual and mental capacities but from being unable to use those abilities to handle difficult situations. If this stage is reached, teachers are serving neither their own interests nor those of the children in the school. They have the sensation of being on a perpetual treadmill with no way off.

Evans (1991) suggests that morale can be talked up or down by senior managers. This is not an argument for more educational administrators. In my view, managers of schools need to have a teaching background, know what makes a good lesson and what makes young people tick. Schools should be run by leading professionals rather than chief executives, and it was this firm conviction that made me decide to look for promotion in order to be in a position to help to raise morale and to have some influence on the management of a school.

It took me three years, many applications and eight interviews before I succeeded in obtaining a deputy headship.

Getting into senior management

Over the three-year period, I began to agree with Morgan and colleagues (1983) who observed that the selection of secondary school headteachers was largely a lottery, in which the applicant had little knowledge of what the selectors were looking for, nor the hidden agenda, micropolitics and prejudices which helped determine their choice. I came to the conclusion that the same was true at deputy headship level.

I quickly learnt that wanting promotion was not enough. Neither was being well qualified, having a successful track record, nor being highly experienced in my current post – all qualities which I believe I possessed. Typically advertisements for deputy headship at secondary level attract over 100 applications. The number of candidates shortlisted is usually between six and 12. A familiar pattern is eight on the first day, reducing to four or less the following day. My dilemma was how to get from being one of over 100 applicants into one of the eight called for interview.

In my case, I flooded the market with applications, at peak times sending off three, four, or even six in a week. About one in six of my applications resulted in an interview. Making so many applications represented a significant but ultimately fruitful investment in time. Even interviews which proved unsuccessful helped focus on areas of whole-school experience which I lacked. Indeed these earlier, unsuccessful interviews were valuable (and free) in-service training.

I have seen colleagues become embittered, blaming their school for giving them poor references, their local authority for being prejudiced against them, and government reforms which have made it impossible for them to gain promotion. Yet the reforms of the last five years affect everyone involved in education: if they represent an impediment to promotion then everyone should be equally disadvantaged. However, I discovered there was a hierarchy of subject specialisms for school senior managers. Ball (1987) describes these as 'patterns of advantage' which tend to privilege certain 'academic' subjects at the expense of the practical and expressive. Hilsum and Start (1974) also discovered that:

If a Headship is the target, then for *teachers of equal experience* the best chances of achieving that goal lie with history, physics, French and maths.

Bennett (1985) describes the restricted opportunities for career development experienced by art teachers, suggesting that because art is a 'low status' subject, like drama and home economics, art teachers are rarely represented at senior management level in schools. What is unclear is whether teachers of these so-called 'low status' subjects are held back because of discrimination against their subject background, whether their own self-perception convinces them that they are unsuitable for senior posts because they lack the relevant qualifications and training, or whether they have a different career orientation from teachers of so-called 'academic' subjects.

I had to acknowledge that coming from a music background did have disadvantages. Not having led a National Curriculum core subject meant I had little experience of chairing meetings, managing resources or leading large teams of colleagues. On the other hand, my experience as a musician has provided me with an awareness of a sense of occasion and performance which are helpful in public events such as open evenings, school functions, and even leading school assemblies.

Lyons (1981) has identified particular strategies used by those actively involved in the pursuit of career advancement. These in-clude a long-term career map, high visibility within the institution, involvement in extra-curricular activity, involvement in educational innovations, and, through political acumen, the acquisition of a sponsor. With the exception of the last, these have been tactics I recognize in my own career, though I would add another, namely evidence of recent relevant study and further qualifications.

Before arriving in the new post

Between my interview in March and my arrival in September I vis-ited the school twice, each time for two days. This was an excellent opportunity to meet new colleagues, learn names and discuss their work. It became possible to develop a feel for the ethos and culture of the school which could not be fully appreciated when attending for interview. During these visits I learnt the names of key academic and pastoral figures, as well as members of the support staff includ-ing the bursar, the school secretaries and the caretakers.

Of particular help was a meeting with the senior management team, which enabled me to crystallize in my mind our respective roles. The head sent me the weekly bulletin and other documents, keeping me in touch with the daily life of the school.

My previous experience had taught me that knowing pupils by name is a powerful management tool. In a school of under 600 pupils it is quite possible to know four out of five pupils or even more, and although this requires a systematic approach and a con-centrated effort, I have found that time spent learning names pays dividends. When walking around the school I can now speak to most pupils by name, and make small talk about sports fixtures, musical events, the morning's assembly. Most of my interaction with pupils around school takes place in a pleasant, relaxed atmos-phere. Before starting my new post I made a conscious decision to be about the school as much as possible, particularly at break times and during lesson changeover. On 'walkabout' I never ignored any suspicious activity, but did my best to avoid public confrontation. Now, when I have to tackle a situation head-on, I make sure it is on my territory (i.e. in my office), in my time, and on my terms (not in front of an audience), although experience has shown that such measures are hardly ever necessary. With time and space of my own, I am able to manage discipline matters in a manner which is productive and largely non-confrontational, a luxury which many teachers do not have.

Teaching remains an important part of my work and is still one of the most rewarding aspects, although I no longer teach principally in my main subject area. Participating in other subjects has helped to give me insight into the curriculum which is not possible by teaching only one subject.

Time

Since I took up the deputy headship, my life has changed radically. One major difference on moving into senior management has been my control over the use of time. This has been an emancipating experience, and has resulted in a significant rise in job satisfaction. In my previous post my time was controlled – by my teaching timetable, by my responsibilities as a form tutor, by rehearsal schedules for services and concerts, and by having to be available to meet visiting music teachers. There was never enough time, and I felt I did not have control of my own agenda. Now, I am able to manage my time. As a deputy head I have a reduced teaching load (12 lessons out of 30), and no day-to-day responsibilities as a head of department or form tutor. I am able to create an agenda of tasks in priority order, and set aside the time to undertake and complete them. Of course there are days when that agenda needs to be revised. If the head is called away on business, leaving me in charge of the school, I may wish to increase my visibility around the school at the expense of the task I was planning to do. The crucial factor is that I can choose to do that, because there is sufficient control of time to re-schedule my day. Previously, as director of music, I could not decide to postpone the carol service until February when the diary was less busy, nor could I cancel a rehearsal which 100 people were expecting to attend.

On moving into senior management I have found the responsibilities encountered are greater than before but different, and in some cases managing potentially conflicting responsibilities can cause tensions. For example, I do have the opportunity to stand back, distance myself, have the possibility to evaluate and reflect, but this conflicts with the need to keep involved in the daily life of the school in order to maintain the confidence of staff, parents and pupils.

Managing new tasks

My job description as deputy head bears little resemblance to my previous existence as a director of music. Apart from teaching, which now forms a much smaller proportion of my work, the tasks are totally different. What makes the transition to deputy headship exceptional, particularly when moving from head of department level, is that overnight I have become in the eyes of colleagues 'the expert', in areas where little previous experience existed. Staff perceive me as someone to whom they can turn for help because of my assumed wide knowledge and experience, though in reality many of my colleagues are inevitably far more experienced than me in their specialist area.

Although not previously a member of a senior management team, I now find myself part of a team of five, being required to chair meetings and to take responsibility for the school during any absences of the head, whether planned or unplanned. This first occurred during my third week in the post, when the head was away at a three-day conference.

No amount of in-service training could have adequately prepared me for these responsibilities, but they had to be faced. I had wanted the responsibility, so now I had to accept it with the appearance of confidence. I knew that I might make mistakes, but whatever happened, I was keenly aware that I must avoid disasters.

Actors, roles and micropolitics

I find I have to play several roles, often simultaneously, and these role expectations differ according to whether it is the head, other colleagues, parents, pupils, the local authority or governors who are making the demands. The term 'role' implies taking on the part of an actor, and on occasions, I feel I am not allowed to be myself, or choose my own words. Ball (1987), Becher (1984), and others refer to actors playing out their roles in the theatre of education – roles which restrict and pattern behaviour, standards and expectations. Hoyle (1986) in *The Politics of School Management* emphasizes the influence of micropolitics on school policy making. He writes that:

> schools are characterized by a network of exchange relationships which constitute a structure perhaps as potent with regard to the organizational character of the school as the formal authority structure.

I have discovered that in the world of micropolitics it is the covert rather than the overt, the influential rather than the powerful, the unwritten rather than the formal arrangement, which hold sway. Micropolitics can be used to promote policies, but also to block and delay, impeding and stifling formal policy decisions, but without demonstrating overt hostility. A deputy's legitimized power derives from the head, but a deputy with micropolitical acumen is in a strong position to rebuff micropolitical moves from other staff, forming a strong ally to the headteacher's authority. As a deputy, my formal authority derives from the head, but as a manager of people, much of what I do is achieved through influence, not power.

Working with the head

Working regularly in proximity to a headteacher has been a new experience for me. Although I enjoyed a close working relationship with my former head, this related principally to my subject area. Many whole school issues were a closed book, and the manner in which decisions were reached was unclear. In my new post I have access to a wide range of information concerning both pupils and staff. On most days I see the head two or three times, usually informally. We share confidential information on a 'need to know' basis, the guiding principle being that if one of us is unavailable the other should be sufficiently briefed to be able to pick up the matter with confidence.

As Lawley (1988) discovered in his study of the role of deputy heads, tensions can arise between heads and their deputies. Healthy conflict is a necessary part of change and development and at times deputies will inevitably need to disagree with the head, albeit judiciously and sensitively. I am fortunate that the head delegates tasks and then leaves them entirely in my hands. Not all heads operate in this way. Thus the responsibility for writing the timetable has been entirely mine; I was left alone to get on with the job. At the same time I know if I requested assistance it would be readily given This large degree of autonomy is a strong contributory factor towards job satisfaction.

Management teams

The very fact that I am part of a management team reflects an approach to school management which has changed greatly in the last thirty years. Morgan et al. (1986) chart the changes in the expectations of headship during this century, from the days when the 'headmaster' held absolute power, to the more recent model of a 'headteacher' who is the leading professional. Schools continue to undergo changes which make them more complex than ever before. They cannot now be managed effectively by one person, hence the evolution of the management team. Though its members may offer differing experiences and viewpoints and may not always agree, a shared sense of values, direction and goals is necessary if a school is to function successfully. In a strong team its members' strengths complement one another. Each member is a team player, and the head is the team captain. Shared values and common aims contribute to a strong, functional management structure.

The senior management team to which I belong comprises the head, two deputies and two senior teachers. All have a significant teaching load. Some would consider a management team of five excessive for a school of under 600 pupils, but this number produces a positive dynamic team. Senior management team meetings have become important arenas of debate, subject to Cabinet-style tensions of the kind described by Lawley (1988), but we have a symbiotic relationship, because we depend on one another to operate effectively. Combined strengths contribute to a strong, functional school culture. Weaknesses cause ineffective management, lack of direction and a weak school culture, which impinges on the work of the classroom teacher and the quality of learning. As a deputy I hope to be able to contribute directly to the effectiveness of the school through relationships with others in the organization. I try to make a point of speaking to *all* staff – teachers, secretaries, the bursar, caretaking and cleaning staff, lunch-time organizers, kitchen staff and technicians whenever I see them, and giving praise where praise is due. Pupils like to be encouraged and so do staff.

Sadly there are those who seem to have very little to say about our schools which is good, yet we are expected to deliver the goods. This inevitably has a damaging effect on morale, but the picture is not altogether gloomy. Despite the plethora of change with which schools are having to cope, positive developments are taking place notwithstanding the obstacles placed in our way.

The National Curriculum has required teachers to rethink not only what they teach and how they teach, but has re-focused their attention on how children learn. Local management of schools has encouraged headteachers, teachers and governors to look more closely at where resources are directed and to formulate development plans as a means of achieving targets.

Conclusions

The pressures on senior management are not less than those I experienced in middle management, but they are different. As a head of department, I was concerned with very many day-to-day responsibilities which could not be avoided. As a deputy head, I have to think on my feet more often, and I am more likely to encounter unfamiliar situations. The stakes are higher, and mistakes will be judged by a wider, more critical audience. On the positive side, my present post does allow me more control over time. I do not work less hard. Most deputies and senior teachers have a substantial teaching load, not necessarily in their main subject area. When posts of this nature attract over 100 applicants the selectors can demand a great deal from the successful candidate.

In an attempt to make an effective transition from middle to senior management I have attempted to formulate my own set of priorities, which are

1 to have a vision of where the school is going and to share that vision with others;
2 to know the pupils and be known by them;
3 to acknowledge that the staff are the most valuable resource in the school, to take time to show they are valued, and to do my best to 'talk up' morale;
4 to remember that if difficult situations arise with a colleague, a personal approach is almost always better than a letter or memo;
5 to remember that life is too short to become depressed about what cannot be achieved, because some targets can never realistically be accomplished;
6 to be proactive not reactive;
7 to manage the agenda (daily, weekly, yearly) and not to lose control over time;
8 to support senior colleagues publicly even when there is private disagreement;
9 to enjoy the job.

In spite of all the problems and responsibilities, I enjoy my work. What gives me greatest satisfaction is seeing my influence – not power – over the life of the school and its members. The teaching profession will never be a sinecure, not for a head, deputy or newly qualified teacher, but there are the occasional rewards which for me still make the job worthwhile. Most of the time!

7

LEAVING THE PROFESSION

Gill Richardson

I recently took early retirement from teaching after a career which began in 1965. I had taught in the state system in junior, middle, grammar, secondary modern schools and in further education and, for the final 13 years, in a comprehensive school. Most of the time I taught English, had been head of a sixth form for a while, and had managed two English departments. While the schools that I worked in varied considerably, they were all places where teachers worked hard to give students a good education. The examination results of my classes at 16 were good and every candidate I taught at A Level passed. I say these things not only because I am proud of them but also because I am going to consider stress in the teaching profession and, since I imagine many of the readers of this chapter are likely to be teachers, I am aiming to pre-empt an occupational assumption – that if I felt stressed I was weak or incompetent, and that it was my fault. There is a strong tendency in teachers to blame themselves when things do not go right and I think that this is one of the causes of stress. In this chapter I shall consider the external factors that contribute to the pressures on teachers, the day-to-day features of the job which is unlike any other job and the pressures that many teachers inflict on themselves.

The phenomenon of teachers feeling undervalued and responsible for most of the ills of society is fairly recent and has filtered through from the government, via the media and the courts, to parents and to pupils themselves. Think for a moment about the way the teachers who taught you would have responded to a parent complaining at a parents' evening that her children will not do homework. Or to a pupil quite openly attributing his or her disruptive behaviour to the lesson being boring. With incredulity, I suspect. But how do most of us react now? We feel guilty; to punish ourselves we stay in detention with the miscreant in an attempt to emphasize the importance of doing homework. Then we go home and try to think of ways of making our lessons more stimulating. I am beginning to think that this is wrong. It would be foolish to suggest that all teachers have the same degree of commitment to the job. Perhaps there was a time when teachers made invalid assumptions about their own power and importance but now we have moved to an unhealthy and opposite extreme. Of course it is right that teachers take on part of the heavy responsibility of preparing children for life, but teachers are not responsible for everything nor should they accept the blame for so many things that go wrong.

Unfortunately, the government manifests all too obviously its lack of faith in the teaching profession. The report of the National Commission on Education, *Learning to Succeed* (1993), makes this explicit when it says that the current mood of distrusting professional educators and relying too much on market forces 'has been carried too far and must be reversed'. Fourteen Education Acts in 14 years have been felt necessary to improve standards and the Secretary of State apparently sees no irony in suggesting, when examination results do improve, that there must be something wrong with the examinations themselves. Most parents and most teachers, bemused though they might be about the detail of some of the legislation, have few complaints about the concept of the National Curriculum or of compulsory regular assessment of pupils and reporting to parents. Two details of the legislation, however, show the lack of faith the government has in teachers, namely the reduction in course work to a fraction of its former self, and the publication of league tables, both of which publicly undermine the professional judgement of teachers and make them susceptible to self-criticism.

English teachers in particular have always been accustomed to course work assessment. Admittedly we often complained about the amount of time we spent on the unpaid moderation of several hundred folders of work each year but, both as a head of department and as a moderator visiting schools in the Manchester area, I was always impressed by the meticulous care that was taken over the exercise. Teachers would agonize over two marks here or there, would argue cases at moderation meetings, would send folders which caused special difficulty to be moderated externally and were always as objective and fair as it was possible to be. For the vast majority of students continuous assessment ensured that they achieved results which reflected their ability and their commitment to the course over two years. However, it seems that the government felt that teachers were in some way cheating or that this way of working was a soft option. Now in order to ensure that standards are upheld, the examination boards have had to regress to a situation where the final examinations take precedence and course work is limited to 20 per cent. English teachers campaigned against this step as vociferously as they could but their campaign became engulfed in a flood of outrage about other more immediate matters, not least the speed with which reforms had to be implemented. The often unrealistic timescale seems to be one of the major causes of weariness in the teaching profession. Changes must happen *now*; lists must be produced *this* year. So the league tables have been compiled from unsophisticated data. London University has devised a rather more skilfully constructed evaluation exercise and compiled a table of 'value added' results. The *Guardian* of 30 November 1993, in publishing these tables, commented in its leader

> the Government's league tables, based purely on raw scores, are not just unfair, but misleading. Clever intakes produce clever results. Crude tables not only camouflage poor performances in affluent suburbs but, worse still, punish highly successful schools who have pushed up standards in deprived areas against the odds.

The information provided in the government's tables, moreover, is based on a system which is shortly to be superseded by the fully implemented National Curriculum. If the Department for Education had been prepared to wait until 1996 before producing the first league tables, they could have demonstrated real achievement instead of merely pointing out that the rich and strong look better on paper than the poor and weak.

As everyone knows, in the present tables, schools with major advantages come out top and schools in disadvantaged areas come out bottom. The National Commission on Education makes some alternative suggestions, noting with disapproval several elements of the content and format of the government tables. It would be so easy to show how schools, wherever they are, increased their students' competence. In 1996 the first year-group to have been ascribed National Curriculum levels in English, Maths and Science at age 14 (Key Stage 3) should reach their final level at age 16 (Key Stage 4). A simple subtraction of the former from the latter would show how much each student had achieved in this two-year period. The results might not be very spectacular – most students would probably have gone up one or two levels in the two years – but schools with even the most difficult intake would have the chance to show that they were as good as some of the more privileged institutions in ensuring their students moved from one level to another. By 1996, however, there could be serious effects on some schools if the tables continue to be published in their present form.

In the first year that league tables were published, my school's intake measured at the age of 13 had 73 per cent of pupils with a reading age below their chronological age but, by the time they were 16, 27 per cent had achieved grades of A–C in GCSE (General Certificate of Secondary Education) English. This is something to celebrate; instead we were the 'worst' school in the area. To come bottom in the league, even if only in one's own local education authority, is to feel not only failure but the threat of impending closure. The sense of failure afflicts the students as well as their teachers. We could not ignore the situation; the newspapers, with a few disclaimers about the inaccuracy of the tables, printed them in full and commented on them as they stood. All we could do was to say, like Boxer in Orwell's *Animal Farm*, we 'must work harder', and we must get better results somehow.

Newspaper opinion seems largely to echo the government's implications about teachers. It seems teachers are ruining children's futures by refusing to administer tests; they are allowing truants to terrorize housing estates; they are left-wing militants who have long holidays, and newspaper readers, many of them parents, absorb these ideas. Teachers have come to believe that they cannot command respect. We tell each other that we have no automatic right to be respected; we have to *earn* respect, but increasingly I begin to question this view. Why should I, or anyone else, accept without question the clearly articulated contempt of a 13-year-old? The kind of disrespect I am referring to is not necessarily a serious breach of discipline or disruptive behaviour. In fact, a young teacher mentioning such an occurrence to a senior member of staff may risk a further loss of self-esteem because it sounds petty in the telling. Little events like this can happen daily, wearing away at teachers' resilience. We almost always look for causes in ourselves: 'I didn't know about the trouble she is having at home'; 'My charisma lapsed for a minute or two'; 'I am losing my sense of humour'. All these things may well be true but, looking back, I do not think I should have accepted all the blame or felt so guilty. Schools themselves could do much more in some cases, particularly for younger members of staff, to create a supportive, and therefore more efficient, working atmosphere. Senior management might aim to ensure that staff *and* pupils have a *right* to mutual respect unless they forfeit that right by insensitive, unprofessional or crass behaviour. A few teachers would undoubtedly be found to have used up their reserve of respect but many more, given truly purposeful and supportive backing, might feel they could get on with the business of teaching and go home feeling lighter of heart at the thought of having done a satisfying day's work.

The final question I should I like to consider is whether teachers contribute to their own sense of inadequacy, and thus stress, by demanding too much of themselves every day. By asking this I am not suggesting that we should be slipshod or negligent or ill-prepared but that we should be realistic about who we are and what we are doing. We can all think back to the teachers who taught us. How many of them though were 'excellent'? Would their excellence be appropriate in the average 1990s comprehensive classroom? Most of them did an adequate job, had the occasional flash of brilliance, usually involved us in the interest they had in their subject and sometimes made us laugh. In many cases the classes they taught were considerably easier to teach than the mixed-ability groups in most comprehensive schools now. Moreover, society's attitude towards them and towards the process of education was largely unquestioning – schools provided pupils with qualifications and with qualifications one could 'get on'. Teaching is no longer concerned merely with instructing and neither the carrot of qualifications nor the stick of corporal punishment, both of which were an easy recourse in maintaining discipline before, now provide an answer to the unmotivated student.

Attitudes towards students have altered immeasurably. Teachers do their best to treat each student as an individual, not simply as a member of a class to be subjugated by threats. Being a teacher is much more complicated than it used to be. Schools demand as much in terms of pastoral commitment as they do in terms of subject skills. Teachers have to summon up immense reserves of resourcefulness, patience, energy and care. A mixed-ability class is often not only mixed in gender; it is mixed socially and ethnically, therefore containing individuals at very different stages of emotional and physical development, with a wide variation of expectations and many potential distractions in its collective mind. It often seems to me remarkable that any lesson goes well in the circumstances and a lesson that feels completely successful is a genuine cause for celebration and self-congratulation.

During my final year in teaching I became the mentor of a licensed teacher and attended a training course for teacher mentors. It was this course that made me wonder about the demands teachers make on themselves. The course was based on the idea that, while it is difficult to analyse what makes a good teacher, there are 12 competences, subdivided into a number of different elements which form the foundation for success. Each month we looked at one competence area in some depth and each month I found myself becoming more depressed. The licensed teacher to whom I was attached was a Music graduate who had been choir master in various churches but had no formal teaching qualification. As it turned out he was a very competent teacher who achieved rapport with his classes, was developing hitherto unsuspected musical skills in quite a few students and giving the rest an experience which was creative and fun. He was able to draw from the cacophony of practical group work sessions little performances which were listened to carefully by the rest of the class and to get the class to comment constructively on each other's work. I was able to point out one or two things he could do which experience had shown me might make his lessons more effective but I was impressed by him as a teacher and probably learnt as much from watching him as he did from me. What we were meant to do, however, was to take each competence area in turn and ascribe to each element a level of awareness. Each area seemed to be held to be of equal importance so it made me consider aspects of teaching that perhaps I had relegated to a lower priority than others. On the other hand, we were ultimately being eased in the direction of adopting a critical attitude instead of being appreciative of our colleague's performance.

Here, for example, was a teacher who formed a choir and a band in a school where these had not existed for some time, and yet was able to put together a Christmas celebration three days after the school production of a musical – at a time when his commitments to his church choir were also reaching a crescendo. It hardly seemed fair or appropriate for me to explore with him how aware he might be of the importance of incorporating cross-curricular themes in his lessons or whether, to be ascribed 'basic proficiency' in his awareness of the environment for learning. I could observe that the music room was 'clean; well-kept; good desk lay-out; attractive, regularly changed posters and children's work; up-to-date notice board'. (To be at Level 5 my own room should have been 'colourful and attractive ... with stimulating, well-mounted, regularly changed display work; well laid out with readily available resource material, artefacts and plants'.) I felt that if there were an advanced teaching diploma, like the advanced driving test, which people could take after several years of practical experience, these criteria would have been relevant but, unless I had concentrated on these requirements to the exclusion of all my other tasks, I might well have failed. Many licensed teachers, moreover, would be feeling exhausted from their first experience of the hourly challenge of large and boisterous classes and the demands of being a form tutor to 28 adolescents.

Do not get me wrong. I do believe that in an ideal world my resource areas would be clearly organized, my monitoring of off-task behaviour would have moved through the strict gradations of 'investigation, counselling, academic help, reprimands and (only then) punishments', and that no-one would ever catch me out on whether I had clear expected outcomes regarding 'values' to be learned in my lesson on how to construct an essay. But I could not put my hand on my heart and say that I never got irritated or even raised my voice at someone *before* counselling them nor discovered that I had left a carefully prepared set of prompt sheets for a lesson in the staff room on the other side of the school. I am sure that it is a valuable exercise to analyse what good teaching is, to show what teachers can do *at their best*, and that we should all aspire to having our drawers tidy at all times, but to hold up such councils of perfection as the basic requirements of the tasks is not realistic or even reasonable. It surely leads to a distressing sense of inadequacy and incompetence.

The National Curriculum for English in its original form had a similarly detailed analysis of what comprised the basic teaching of English and, however hard English teachers tried to re-phrase its stipulations to make it sound comprehensible, it was almost impossible to conduct assessments or to write reports that would really convey the truth to parents about their children's progress. I believe that even the best and most experienced teachers, who had taught English both effectively and joyously, felt pangs of guilt about their inability to deliver and assess English according to the fine detail of the English Statements of Attainment.

I have come to the conclusion that there are ways in which teachers can help themselves to hold stress at bay. Having time to talk to one another is one of the most effective ways of defusing stress. It allows people to share self-doubt, express anxiety about their competence, and exchange ideas they are really proud of, with someone whose job it is to be interested. One of the major bonuses of the licensed teacher–mentor relationship was the hour every week which was timetabled simply to talk.

Clearly, the school has an obligation to create a climate within which such confidences can be exchanged, if teachers are not to feel threatened. A well-planned system of appraisal which is sensitive to the needs of the individual school can lead to strong professional bonds being forged and to teachers feeling that someone else is taking a genuine interest in their future. It might help to investigate how successfully the school's support system works, carefully re-move the sticking plasters covering wounded self-esteem and see what has caused the injuries. The common format for appraisal is an initial meeting, lesson observation and information gathering, the appraisal interview, the report and a review. Even as early as the initial interview it is often clear that simply having time to talk about the concerns one feels about the job and the future are a tremendous release to some teachers. This is not to say that we do not normally talk to each other but staffroom talk is often simply social or mundane – even negative at times – and in meetings there is often so much business to be done that individual concerns cannot be properly dealt with. Appraisal meetings, however, have a large DO NOT DISTURB notice on the door and the time is seriously devoted to us as individuals. Assuming that the pairing for the process has been done with tact, both the appraiser and the appraisee can confront and try to overcome perceived difficulties. Fewer teachers these days are disconcerted about having other members of staff in their rooms when they teach, but even so lesson observations possibly seem daunting at first. They can, however, have some unexpectedly positive outcomes. Even the most experienced teachers can be surprised and delighted at the work they observe being done. The discussion which follows the observation is often remarkably pro-ductive and reveals how much the majority of teachers take their own skills, knowledge and values for granted.

Stress is not merely the effect of working hard. Many people, myself included, have worked many hours a day for many years. Stress is caused by feeling bad about oneself and constantly being made aware of one's inadequacy even though one is actually quite good at the job. Very few teachers are saints with an endless capacity to take the blame for the cracks that are appearing in our society. The vast majority of us are hard-working and committed and would be very satisfied if our students, the parents of our students, the management of our schools and the government, would say a little more often 'You're doing a good job'. They, and we, might even begin to believe it.

8

REVISITING CLASSROOMS

Ken Bryan

What we perceive to be significant about particular events or processes is powerfully influenced by the context in which they are located. This recognition, although by no means novel, is especially pertinent to what we consider to be good or effective teaching. Schools reflect the wider values of society; classrooms are nested in schools, and teachers and pupils continually modify their relationships in the light of their perception of what happens in individual classrooms. Pupils and teachers bring their prior experiences of life into schools, and it is from the complex interplay of these and other considerations that judgements are formed as to what is a good school and what is good teaching.

In this chapter, I seek to explore whether my perceptions of what counts as a good school and good teaching have changed during 30 years or so as a teacher of pupils, student teachers, in-service teachers and other adults. I shall be recalling events from both my early career and my present position. I am not seeking to provide a description or explanation of how my professional thinking and practice have changed during the intervening years; merely I am attempting sketches of then and now. This exploration is one aspect of what I have come to regard as an exercise in professional self-development.

Today both the macro and micro climates in which teaching and learning are located and assessed appear to be very different from the end of the 1950s where I begin.

Initially I give some brief biographical detail to provide a context for reflection on my professional thinking and practice. There is a sense in which I became a teacher by accident. As a sixth form pupil I knew that what I wanted to do was to become a forensic scientist. I did not expect to begin my university studies until a year after completing my A Levels. The headteacher of my grammar school suggested I spend the time as an unqualified teacher in a nearby secondary modern school which at that time had a serious staff shortage. As part of my 'in-service training' the headteacher of this secondary modern school required that I should write an essay on what I considered to be the purposes of secondary schooling and comment on the extent to which his school was achieving those aims. I shall quote from this essay shortly. In the event I began my university studies ten weeks or so after starting teaching.

During my first year as a science student I discovered that I was colour blind and had difficulty in identifying the colour of precipitates, and so on. At the end of the year I changed course from science to arts, and began to study education, which embraced psychology and philosophy, history and mathematics. That year of studying chemistry, together with my subsequent undergraduate studies in the social sciences, provided me with the essential foundation for an understanding of 'what counts' as theory and evidence. I doubt whether there are more important considerations in today's debate as to whether or not education is 'working'.

After graduation and teacher training I returned to the same secondary modern school as a qualified teacher. Re-reading an essay written during my training entitled 'Purposes of Secondary Schooling' reveals my concern with five issues: selection at 11-plus, pupil–teacher relationships, the differentiation of pupils within schools, the desirability or otherwise of school uniform, and problems associated with the school leaving age which permitted pupils to end their schooling at the end of the term in which they reached 15. With the exception of the latter, all these issues are still current. Not surprisingly, my judgement of what is deemed to be good practice has changed, to use a phrase beloved of politicians, 'in the light of experience'.

Although I argued that the selection of pupils for different forms of secondary schooling at 11-plus was premature, and the procedures used were manifestly subject to significant error, I maintained that 'it was the most efficient yet devised'. I endorsed selective schooling and concluded that, despite the difficulties associated with changing schools at 11, to delay the judgement further would present 'many complications in the planning of grammar and technical syllabuses'. I also came down in favour of school uniform. On reflection I am satisfied that I was echoing the consensus view of most of my colleagues. At least the headteacher agreed: in his view I 'showed a surprising awareness and a sound appreciation of values'! Little did I realize then that twenty years later I would be a convinced advocate of comprehensive secondary schooling.

Not surprisingly in 1959 I found it easier to teach the 'top' (A and B) rather than the 'lower' (C and R) streams. The comments I made in my essay were specific to the maths and science which I was teaching. I noted that pupils' attainment in science which had a problem-solving focus was higher, and that they had more choice in how to proceed than in maths which was closely tied to the textbook. Overall the 'top' classes were 'a delight to teach' and 'I was genuinely surprised at the general standard of the "A" stream'. The extent to which my grammar school experience had, intentionally or not, inflated my own and other sixth formers' perceptions of standards and played down the achievements of the nearby 'sec. mod.' can only remain speculation.

Pupil–teacher relationships were positive within clearly perceived, but undefined limits. My notes refer to co-operation and familiarity within a framework of mutual respect. Inevitably there were classroom cynics, but their influence on staff morale seemed negligible. Most of the staff, whose ages ranged from nearing retirement to the very young qualified and unqualified, were committed to the school as an institution with a particular identity which was expressed most evidently in the school's sporting activities.

My formal academic and teacher training sensitized me early to how the 'light' might be filtered and polarized by 'experience'. I learned much from my early colleagues; the knowledge and skills they possessed were invaluable, particularly in relation to administration procedures and classroom coping strategies. Other advice I was happy to discard rapidly. I often wonder what has happened to one pupil whom I was told 'was not born to die a natural death'!

Although several of my early colleagues guided me on the sequencing of material and how I might 'teach' particular topics, no one prompted me to ask why a pupil's first question, after what I considered to be an erudite explanation and demonstration of the reasons for day and night was, 'Sir, are you married?', or to reflect on why another pupil, who subsequently admitted authorship to me, wrote on the blackboard before the first lesson I took with his class, 'Bryan is a f***ing git'. I felt then to have informed my colleagues of such events and testimonials would have been construed as weakness on my part. To argue that it is not the school's first or second priority to train, let alone educate teachers will probably be considered as special pleading from a current college lecturer. I doubt, however, if my interest in and concern for what goes on in children's minds would have been stimulated by a longer period as an unqualified teacher. I still contend that to study and reflect on ways in which children think and learn, and to be able to evaluate evidence is a distinguishing characteristic of a good teacher – and such a grounding is likely to be best provided outside the school setting.

In those early days thematic approaches to curriculum planning were genuinely supported by many members of staff. We knew that comparisons between grammar and secondary modern schools were wholly inappropriate. The boys' grammar school admitted pupils with an IQ of about 120-plus, the local education authority (LEA) had a small secondary technical school, so our intake embraced what Newsom was to term 'Half our Future'. Although it was clearly in the school's interest to develop different and distinctive curricula for most of its pupils, the more academically able were entered for ULCI (Union of Lancashire and Cheshire Institutes) exams which were subject based.

With hindsight I can see why in the early 1960s I regarded the school as the locus for decision making in education. The curriculum was seen by David Eccles, the then Minister of Education, as the teachers' 'secret garden'. Prime Minister Harold MacMillan had recently convinced the people 'that they had never had it so good', youth unemployment as a social problem did not exist. For those pupils who found school 'dead boring' there was unskilled work, if not always apprenticeships. As teachers we could recommend the local 'Tech.' to fourth year pupils who made classroom life difficult. Maintaining school rolls, and hence our jobs, was not a problem.

In 1965 I was appointed head of the history department in a mixed secondary modern school with a roll of approximately 600 pupils. Probably I was promoted early and quickly because I was a graduate in a sector of schooling that was composed then of mostly certificated teachers. At the time of my appointment there was no formal scheme of work and so my first priority was to bring a sense of identity to the department by collaboratively devising a new syllabus. Content was selected to achieve aims and objectives which we judged to reflect good practice in history teaching. No external constraints were imposed on what we should select. Indeed, since there were few text and reference books in the school we were not tempted to construct the syllabus around existing resources! My concern then, which remains now, was how our constructions of the nature and structure of the subject should influence how history is taught and learned. The freedom to choose both the content and the approach to history teaching later gave us the opportunity and incentive to develop some exciting work with Certificate of Secondary Education (CSE) Mode Three syllabuses.

Soon after my appointment the school was subject to a full general inspection by Her Majesty's Inspectorate (HMI). The report that followed referred to thoughtful discussions which augured well for the future. The language of HMI reports then was very different from what it is now. Their report included statements such as 'human relations of unusual quality', a headteacher who was 'courageous and enterprising with a buoyant personality', 'shrewd and zealous teaching', 'pupils who are pleasant to meet, speak well and readily . . . [and] . . . give a very good impression of mature, sensible young people'. Surely comments such as these carry more conviction than 'satisfactory', 'above/below average', 'poor' and 'good', which are cited in the current manual for the inspection of schools issued by the Office for Standards in Education (OFSTED).

Of course it was not all 'wine and roses'. Always there were pupils who saw no point in school, however hard we tried to stimulate their interest. To maintain discipline in the classroom was then, and I believe still is, a first level of competency for acceptance by one's peers. By no means were all parents supportive, but the unambiguous advice I received from one father – 'if our Len give you any more trouble, you tan his arse, and when he gets home I'll give another one to show him I'm behind you' – remains vivid. I did not then, and do not now, see this kind of support as a solution to disaffected pupils. But the context was different: most of my colleagues felt that parents generally shared teachers' concerns; that they were professionals, admittedly relatively more lowly paid then than now, who had the competence to decide what to teach and how, and that they had a legitimate authority to insist on pupils' compliance, even if that was not always achieved.

It was from this limited, but professional optimistic base that I moved into teacher education at the beginning of the 1970s. From the middle of that decade onwards I remained in fairly regular contact with schools and teachers, teaching for short blocks of time in various schools as part of my teacher training commitment and my research into pupils' and teachers' experiences of the middle years of schooling. Involvement in higher education at a time of expansion brought several undoubted opportunities and privileges. Not only did I have the chance to work with teachers and pupils in a variety of settings, but I became involved in curriculum development and teacher education for other professionals. The parallels are illuminating.

Towards the end of the 1980s I was asked by the then Director of

Nurse Education of a nearby school of nursing if I would assist some of his colleagues to draft a course submission to the validating body because the school was experiencing difficulty in securing the necessary course approval. As a result of this initial contact I was asked some months later by a member of the validating body, the English National Board for Nursing and Midwifery, if the College of Higher Education in which I worked would consider providing a Certificate in Education course for teachers of nurses because at that time there was a perceived need for such a programme. I was advised by the professional officers of the Board that they were committed to the principles of adult learning in nurse education and to student nurses taking on an active part in the planning of their professional knowledge and skill acquisition. These principles must be embodied in the proposed programme.

When I had secured the institutional approval to begin the development of this course, I explained to another Director of Nurse Education in the region that I, as a non-nurse whose only experience of nursing had been as a hospital in-patient, was at a considerable disadvantage because I had no experience of the culture of nurses in training which I considered to be essential to an understanding of their needs. Obviously as a school teacher, I had been a pupil previously; as a student teacher I had experience of a teacher training institution, and as someone who was associated with aspects of training within the prison service, I had been in several prisons, although not as a prisoner! However, knowledge 'about' is a poor substitute for knowledge 'of'.

It was agreed that I would spend part of the 1988 summer vacation in the company of student nurses during their foundation block. As far as they and their tutors were concerned I was a potential mature entrant to nursing; no details of my status or position were given. My purpose was to get as near as practicable to the lived experience of these student nurses. When allocated to a midwifery placement, which involved the examination of an abnormal placenta, the midwifery tutor asked me 'whether I could cope with the blood?' My answer, which appeared to surprise her was to ask why she thought I might not 'be able to cope with the blood'. She replied that it was not unusual for fathers to faint when present at the birth of their children. From later feedback I learned that she was unused to having a question answered by another question.

The purpose of this anecdote is to illustrate two points: first, that the imputed gap between the rhetoric of teacher training and the realities of life in classrooms is not peculiar to mainstream schools and secondly, to emphasize that an understanding of institutional settings is an essential component in the processes of teaching and learning. However 'progressive' the rhetoric of the validating body's professional officers, the lived experience of many nurses in training was that hospital staff remained hierarchical in their definition of roles and functions. I must emphasize that I am not saying that the guidelines given by the professional officers were misleading or inappropriate; indeed schools of nursing, as they were then, were seen by themselves and by their institutional masters, especially the Department of Health and Social Security and the Treasury, as the proper agencies for initiating and sustaining necessary and desirable change. That nurses are being encouraged to become reflective practitioners within the context of higher education rather than being merely the subservient handmaidens of medical practitioners seems to me to be real professional development.

What does appear paradoxical is that it is the same government which is promoting substantially college based Project 2000 courses for nurses, which is also insisting that the training of school teachers must be undertaken almost exclusively within schools and not in 'ivory towers'. Most of the student nurses and qualified nurses with whom I have been working over the past four years tell me that informed reflection, which is a prerequisite for professional self-development requires substantial 'off the job training'.

Whether the recent and substantial cutback in recruitment to nursing, with the consequent reduction in the need for more highly qualified nurse teachers, is a result of inadequate personnel planning or the unexpressed, but intended, outcome of a policy that permitted nurses to over-specify their professional knowledge and roles so that they could be substituted by less qualified and lower paid helpers, is beyond the scope of this essay. What is pertinent is that national policies concerning the funding and provision of teacher and nurse education are having a direct impact on what is taught and how.

My most recent experience of teaching full-time in schools was during the second half of the summer and the first half of the autumn terms, 1993. My intentions were twofold: to up-date my 'recent, relevant and successful' experience in both primary and secondary schools, and to initiate an action research project into pupils' experience of primary-secondary transfer. Although the secondary school in which I worked had well-established links with its main partner primaries, the headteacher had earlier commented to me that continuity of curriculum could be improved in some areas. Certain departments in his school operated a 'fresh start' policy which seemed repetitious and inefficient for some pupils.

During the planning stage I visited the three main partner primary schools to ascertain what Year 6 pupils (that is pupils in their last year) would be doing during the summer term. I also identified

with the heads of the maths and religious education (RE) departments in the secondary school the topics with which the first year
(Year 7) pupils would begin. It was agreed that I would take full
responsibility for the Year 6 class in one of the primary schools, and
teach maths and RE to most or all the Year 7 pupils when they
started secondary school. Maths which was taught in ability sets was
chosen to represent a subject which is seen as highly structured and
sequenced. The content of RE was seen as more open to negotiation
and was taught in mixed ability groups. I set out to see whether
curricular continuity was being achieved more successfully in either
of these cases. This aspect of the project is still in progress.

Teaching in these two schools enabled me to explore in some
detail with staff and pupils what they were doing and why, as well
as to record my reflections on contemporary life in classrooms and
schools. When teaching in the primary school especially, my lesson
notes were designed to achieve clearly stated aims and objectives. A
re-reading of these planning notes shows a concern to develop
concepts and skills. In mathematics, for example, 'At the end of this
unit of work most pupils will be able to (i) state the meaning of
scale, (ii) explain the meaning of scale, (iii) read scale drawings and
(iv) prepare scale drawings.' In English I wanted pupils to '(i) formulate precisely-worded questions to one another, (ii) record the other's
answers, and (iii) express questions and answers in appropriate form
using the correct punctuation for the reporting of direct speech'.
The RE topic negotiated between myself and the staff at both the
primary and secondary schools was 'Signs and Symbols'. My stated
objectives were for pupils '(i) to identify particular signs in school,
street and church, (ii) to explain the meaning of these particular
signs, and (iii) to identify and distinguish between signs and symbols in church'.

Surprisingly, in retrospect, my lesson evaluations give a dispropor-
tionate emphasis to pupils' negative dispositions and motivation,
for example 'unduly attention seeking', 'easily distracted and dis-
tracting', 'if she applied herself she would achieve much more accurate work'. My observations on pupils' reading and mathematics
attainment are much more skill specific: 'has problems enunciating
words ending in -tion' and 'problems with subtraction when set
in difference format'. I make no reference at all to the relevance of
content. I shall refer to this issue again *vis-à-vis* my reflection on
teaching in the secondary school.

Discussions with staff were wholly informal and in no sense can
the following observations be fairly described as the outcome of
structured or unstructured interviews; they are a summary of extended
staffroom conversations over a seven-week period. The National

Curriculum and its impact on teachers' professional lives was the principal theme running through our discussions. This was to be expected. Although the majority of staff could 'live with' subjects being the basis for curriculum planning, it was the likely impact of this upon how they might have to teach and organize their day which seemed to threaten their professional practice. Certainly there were substantial resource implications. Where there were discernible differences in emphasis, these seemed to centre around age; the older members of staff (late forties and early fifties), with the exception of the headteacher, were more at ease with a 'subject' basis. In one sense this is surprising in that they were trained in the 'liberal' 1960s.

Although the main focus of my work in the secondary school was aspects of curriculum continuity with Year 7, I taught pupils in other years to provide me with a full (i.e. 85 per cent) timetable commitment. Specification of content was the top priority with the staff whose classes I taught. Both maths and RE teachers were explicit in their concern that I should 'cover' the specified topics in the time allowed. Specific chapters of the Northern Maths Project scheme were to be covered in two-week blocks. Perusal of my lesson notes shows that my aims and objectives were set out clearly, but they were generally less precise and incremental than those I had written for teaching in the primary school, for example 'estimate to the nearest whole unit measures of length, temperature, weight and time'. I suspect that the reason for this was that my lesson planning derived almost exclusively from the set textbooks. Another distinguishing feature of my teaching notes for secondary pupils was that I set down more extensively possible alternative expositions for particular topics. For the more academically able sets, my post-lesson observations refer largely to variations in the pace with which particular pupils worked and the levels of accuracy which they achieved.

In these descriptions of classroom life 'then' and 'now' the importance of the changing context which conditioned teachers' perceptions of teaching emerges as especially significant. Secondary school teachers have long been sensitive to the constraints imposed by external examination boards. In this sense the constraints imposed by the National Curriculum are not new. Thus the secondary staff's concern for me to work briskly through the specified content was understandable and to be expected. My priority to provide sufficient evidence, including material additional to that in the published schemes, to enable pupils to form a sound conceptual understanding, derives from my long involvement in teacher education where the theoretical underpinnings to learning have traditionally been stressed. Although the secondary school had not participated in Key

Stage 3 trials (at age 14), the requirements for external testing before the General Certificate of Secondary Education (GCSE) have, I believe, intensified teachers' anxiety to 'cover' the content. Both what pupils learn and how they learn it is becoming increasingly directed from outside the school.

As in the primary school, the anxiety about testing centred around the potential comparative uses to which data might be put. Both schools were anxious to increase the recruitment of pupils from the relatively small middle-class sectors of their traditional catchment areas. Factors external to the school affect both teachers and pupils, if in different ways. Since I had not been in regular contact with secondary schools for nearly 10 years, to me the most notable change was the depressed level of motivation among significant numbers of the middle ability range, especially among 18 year-old school leavers. The lack of job opportunities has, in my view, a palpable effect on pupils' aspirations and approach to schooling. To many, return to school is seen as preferable to a youth training placement; pupils remain with their friends and feel less threatened with the familiar. Neither option, however, holds out many real job opportunities for them.

The charge that the nation's schools are failing the nation's young people is not a new one and tends to recur at times of economic crisis (Dale *et al.*, 1981). When teaching 15 year-olds in the 1960s, I was told by apprentice training officers that schools should ensure that leavers possessed the general skills of literacy and numeracy; industry would teach the necessary technical knowledge. Now that the profit margins which financed such in-house training have been massively reduced, once again it is the schools' responsibility to equip the young for the world of work. Both teachers and pupils with whom I have recently discussed the purposes of secondary schooling are confused as to how the essentially traditional curriculum, as specified in the National Curriculum, will provide the appropriate knowledge and skills for the 1990s and beyond.

What conclusions, then, do I draw from these sketches of life in classrooms? As with photographs they represent what seemed significant or interesting at the time. That significance or interest has inevitably been re-interpreted in the light of experience. Each one of us tries to make sense of our world, but in so doing we view that world partially. The notion of 'image' is helpful in my con- ceptualization of my professional world. Images both describe what I see as important and focus my thinking on the imputed realities behind them; images convey and generate meanings. To ask myself how my image of 'teacher as practitioner' has changed since I started teaching is pertinent in this exercise of professional reflection. Like all teachers, I have an image of good and difficult pupils and classes, and I have formed views as to what professional knowledge is central to everyday life in classrooms.

I concur with most teachers that to provide knowledge of those aspects deemed necessary for adult life is an important function of schooling, but as my career has developed, I have increasingly emphasized the 'how' rather than the 'what' of learning, not least because the requirements of society change more readily than do pupils' needs. Sir Joshua Fitch said in 1865 at a lecture at the York Institute: 'Now I do not know a meaner way of estimating the work of knowledge than to ask what is the use of it in the business of life.' I agreed with this view when I first read it nearly 30 years ago and I still do, now perhaps even more so.

My image of the ideal class and how I seek to achieve it has also changed. Although my early concerns with order and control are still important to my professional image, they now have a lower profile. Presumably this is because coping strategies have been routinized and I am not regularly working with pupils who attend under compulsion. If my classroom control is challenged, this becomes *a* test but not *the* test of competence. Now I conceptualize it as a school issue; I raise it with senior staff and discuss it with pupils in terms of how they can be seen as constructing their own failure and fulfilling their teachers' expectations. What is intended as an act of rebellion becomes an act of conformity. Classroom discipline and control are no longer private issues.

For the greater part of my career I have been involved in teacher education. I emphasize 'education' rather than 'training' because I encourage the students and teachers with whom I work to address the question of what professional knowledge they see as essential to their day-to-day work, and why they need it. To me, theory is not a set of procedures that can be applied as deemed appropriate to specific situations. If it is, I should still be looking for the relevant reference as to how to respond to pupils who write 'Bryan is a f***ing git' on the blackboard, or more recently a pupil who told me that she was not doing any work in my lesson. Rather I see theory as a coherent pattern of ideas within which I can interpret class-room life and justify the actions I have taken and propose to take. For me, professional knowledge is constantly being re-created. If I lose my sensitivity to the processes of re-creation then I shall cease to be a competent teacher, let alone a thinking one.

Part three

MOVING TO

LOCAL MANAGEMENT

9

NOT ALL PLAIN SAILING

Peter Swientozielskyj

Introduction

The Local Management in Schools (LMS) Initiative, which is a requirement of the Education Reform Act of 1988, was designed to give schools more control over their own affairs and this initiative has been welcomed by many schools who saw advantages in being able to make decisions without being constrained by local education authority (LEA) policies and procedures, to decide their own priorities, devise workable strategic plans, and respond quickly to emergencies.

Most schools hope to achieve a balance of age and experience among their teachers, but this is not always possible. An above-average age staff, or a too-high ratio of teachers on promoted posts can cause havoc over the control of the budget.

Schools which are struggling to remain within their cost limits will also be faced with the additional problems of finding the cash to take account of increases in pay. The pay rise of 2.9 per cent awarded in 1994 sounds little enough considering the ever-increasing range of duties facing teachers, but knowledge that the government has no intention of providing the money for the increase has caused consternation in LEAs, schools, and among governing bodies.

The Times Educational Supplement of 11 February 1994 addressed

the issue of inadequate budgets in schools and drew attention to the
findings of studies carried out by the Audit Commission and the
Institute of Manpower Studies. Their findings are not encouraging.

Many education authorities are not going to be able to fund this
rise in full, and may have been unprepared for its size. John
Patten's generosity, therefore, could simply represent an additional cost on school budgets to be paid for by pupils taught in
larger, shabbier, less well-equipped classrooms or by teachers
who lose their jobs; a funny old reward for 'sustained and con-
scientious efforts'.

A timely report from the Institute of Manpower Studies this
week casts new light on those school budgets. After questioning
1,600 heads and deputies throughout the country the IMS has
discovered that nearly one school in five overspent its budget in
1991–92. That was even before last year's underfunded salary
settlement. In secondary schools the rate was even worse: one
school in four.

This is double the rate found by the Audit Commission's study,
Adding Up the Sums. That more limited survey, based on just 100
schools in nine local authorities, suggested nine per cent of
schools had bust their budgets.

The IMS survey found 18 per cent had and that nearly one
in five of these – including a quarter of the secondary schools
– was actively considering opting out. If these are typical of
the country as a whole, that would mean something like 1,400
primaries and 800 secondaries were seriously thinking of opting
out even before they were landed with the latest pay burdens.

(Bevan and Barber 1994)

My school did not wish to opt out but at the time this chapter
was writen, the difficulties we were experiencing resulted in the
governors balloting the parents for their views on moving towards
grant maintained status.

Problems, problems, problems

I know that some schools have found that LMS has enabled them
to achieve budget surpluses which have allowed them to provide
additional support for pupils and to upgrade accommodation and
equipment. However, my own school has not been so fortunate and
the move to LMS has caused genuine hardship and constant worry
as to how essential expenditure can be funded.

The school emerged as a result of reorganizations, mergers and
school closures necessitated by falling rolls. Staff of the affected

schools faced a series of disruptions and anxieties and the trauma of having to apply for a greatly reduced number of jobs. Some teachers took advantage of the early retirement terms, but those of us who could not or did not wish to retire, found ourselves in the unenviable position of being in competition with each other for posts in the newly created school.

The LEA has always had a 'no redundancy' policy and over the years implemented what now has to be acknowledged as a generous approach to the award of allowances. As a result, the new school has found itself in the position of having a high proportion of promoted staff, not all of whom now carry responsibilities to justify the salary level.

The first three years of the new school have been difficult. During the first year, we operated on a 'partially delegated' budget. This meant that the school had control over its own budget and all aspects of running the school *except staffing costs*. However, once the school moved to fully delegated status, we became responsible for staffing costs and were open to the full effects of LMS. In this three-year period, the budget deficit rose to a frightening level and this had an enormous impact on all aspects of running the school.

One could argue that the seeds of this financial disaster were planted at reorganization. The staffing structure allocated to the new school was generous and therefore costly. It consisted of a headteacher, three deputies, four senior teachers, 12 curriculum area managers (head of department equivalent) with each department carrying allowances for equal opportunities and special needs. In addition to this, pastoral teams had five members of staff on allowances – a total of 49 promoted posts out of a staff of 69 for a school of only 1000 pupils. Perhaps the effects of the LEA's 'no redundancy' policy, the generous staffing ratio in the new school, and the full implications of staffing costs were not faced at a critical stage, though even now it is difficult to see what could have been done at the time to avoid the necessary salary expenditure which accounted for 85 per cent of the total budget.

It became clear that action had to be taken to improve the situation and a decision was taken to carry out a curriculum audit in order to identify exactly how many teachers were needed to cover the curriculum requirements. The audit was a protracted affair which rumbled on for much of the early part of 1992. There had been much disagreement over procedures between the LEA and the teacher associations, which resulted in the exercise being carried out twice. The anxieties this caused had an adverse effect on staff morale and had a knock-on effect throughout the school.

It was probably inevitable that the audit would demonstrate that

we had too many teachers and that some would have to go, but the
size of the operation was startling. Sixteen teachers left since the
school was founded in 1989. In 1992, five were 'invited' to leave,
four of whom obtained posts elsewhere and one left the profession
altogether. The remaining 11 either decided to take early retirement
or decided there was little future in the school and that it was in
their own interests to make other plans. Most obtained promoted
posts in other schools.

As staff left and were not replaced, the number of 'minority' subjects
was reduced and as a result the options programme was drastically
reduced. The pupil–teacher ratio deteriorated from 1:15 in 1990 to
1:18 in 1993. The ratio was generous in 1990 due to the one year
when the school operated on split sites, but in 1991, the split site
arrangements ceased. Teachers found the increased class sizes, particularly in practical subject areas and the ever-present worry about
possible further redundancies stressful. Staff absences on sick leave
increased and during 1993, three teachers had illnesses which lasted
more than six months. Because of the financial situation of the
school, supply teachers were not always brought in and increasingly
we had to cover for absent colleagues. Classes were doubled up on
occasions to save on supply cover costs and to give staff their precious
non-contact time. Many teachers lost between 20 to 30 non-contact
sessions over the year and this of necessity reduced the time available
for preparation of National Curriculum programmes of study, the
development of the new assessment arrangements and updating of
specialist subjects. We all became desperately tired and there was a
general lack of willingness to take on additional duties. The teaching
environment did little to raise our spirits. School buildings had for
some time been in a poor state of repair. Many window frames were
rotten and were in urgent need of replacement. The whole school
needed painting, floor coverings were worn and the school had a
generally shabby and run-down appearance which was unlikely to
encourage parents to think ours was the best school for their children.
The poor state of the school buildings was further compounded by
attempts to save costs of cleaning. When the school was first built
there were 16 cleaners; at the time this chapter was written there
were eight and plans were afoot to reduce this number to six. That
would inevitably have meant that classrooms would be cleaned on
alternate days rather than on a daily basis.

It was calculated that it cost £7250 annually to heat the school's
swimming pool and when it was discovered that urgent repairs
needed to be carried out, we had no alternative but to close it.

During the 1992/3 academic year, there were changes at senior
management level, and since then further vigorous efforts have been

made to resolve once and for all the financial situation of the school. The early retirement of one of the deputy heads resulted in a 'surplus' of £16,500 on the 1992/3 budget, which the LEA expected to retain to reduce the size of the school deficit. However, the governors and the headteacher argued forcibly against this and finally succeeded in retaining this sum in order for much-needed repairs and alterations to be carried out. Many discussions have taken place with the LEA and the general stance has been that the school *cannot* pay back rather than *will not* pay back. It has been argued that the LEA should either have maintained responsibility for the fabric of the building, or handed it over in good repair if the school was expected to carry out major repairs and refurbishment out of its budget. The problem of the maintenance of the school buildings has not yet been resolved.

Resolution of the problems caused by the large number of staff on promoted posts has proved to be even more difficult. The governors and the LEA put forward a scheme which would have involved all of us being made redundant, a new staffing structure introduced, and the whole staff being required to reapply for new positions. This Draconian approach was finally abandoned and though it is acknowledged that restructuring will be necessary, it is hoped it can be achieved through yet more early retirements and by 'negotiation'.

It is difficult to give an accurate picture of the effect the financial problems have had on teachers. The introduction of the National Curriculum required a major curriculum and assessment review. We responded to the best of our abilities to the many demands for reform and greater accountability, and I honestly believe we have done our best for the children in our care. Teachers who have been fortunate enough to work in a stable environment and with adequate resources to enable them to deliver the curriculum efficiently are fortunate – and I am aware of the fact that not all schools have had to face problems of the kind I have described. However, a good many have, and the increased stress levels of many staff are only too apparent from the numbers of well-respected heads and teachers who have sought early retirement.

Though plans are now afoot to simplify the National Curriculum and to remove some of the more extreme elements, the harsh realities of LMS are here to stay and we shall all have to learn to live with the economics. Perhaps once the major restructuring of staff in the school has been achieved and the size of the senior management team reduced, the school may begin to move towards a more stable and less stressful state. The drive towards accountability in education is long overdue, but schools like mine have found themselves in an untenable position because they were not starting with a clean slate.

The 1992/93 Annual Report of Her Majesty's Chief Inspector of Schools, *Standards and Quality in Education* states:

> There are some fine managers and inspiring leaders in our schools. Despite this, some characteristics of an effective management system are slow to take root: there is a clear and urgent need for improvement. Both in schools with Local Management and, even more so, in the self-governing grant-maintained schools, managers are coming to terms with what it means to control a substantial delegated budget. The more energetic – entrepreneurial – of them have not been slow to exploit their opportunities or to use their new-found powers to carry out their day-to-day responsibilities effectively and efficiently. Nevertheless, there are widespread weaknesses when it comes to longer-term planning. Despite the increasing prominence given to producing School Development Plans, these do not always take the vital step of matching the process of drawing up budgets to educational priorities and ensuring that resources are harnessed to improved quality of teaching and learning.
>
> (Office for Standards in Education (OFSTED) 1993)

Conclusions

The on-going financial crisis has made it difficult for the school and its governors to draw up realistic development plans. The headteacher has found it difficult to carry out his role as an educational leader when there have been so many demands related to the management of the budget, and the question inevitably arises as to whether the financial management of schools should be in the hands of teachers or of professional administrators. I have no wish to be an accountant. I *chose* to be a teacher and at one stage I looked forward to having the opportunity of moving up the ladder and eventually being in a position to influence the way a school was managed. I no longer have such an ambition. If I stay in the teaching profession, I shall continue to do my job as a teacher to the best of my ability, but I have no desire to spend my time struggling to balance the books and being in the position of possibly having to make what may be educationally unsound decisions in order to keep the school afloat.

It would be unfair (and untrue) to suggest that all our problems have been caused by LMS. As I hope I have made clear, the original inheritance of a too large and above average age staff, a high proportion of teachers on promoted posts and the poor state of the school buildings have all contributed to our difficulties. However, I do not believe our position is unique. I should hate to think I have to spend the rest of my life in a school where the budget drives the curriculum. I would hope we never reach that stage, though my own experience increasingly leads me to the sad view that the budget-driven curriculum is likely to be the model for the future.

10

GOVERNORS AND TEACHERS:

THE COSTS OF LOCAL

MANAGEMENT IN SCHOOLS

Ann Hanson

In the last chapter, Peter Swientozielskyj describes the difficulties facing his school after the introduction of Local Management in Schools (LMS). As a parent governor of a small primary school, I encountered many similar problems and, with the headteacher and governor colleagues, struggled to lessen the impact on teachers and pupils not only of LMS, but also of the series of reforms introduced at what seemed at the time to be breakneck speed. The Education Acts of 1986 and 1988 brought about fundamental changes in the structure of education, but the impact on governing bodies was not really felt until the beginning of 1989. Maybe this was due in some part to a Canute-like belief that these groups could still meet three times a year, listen politely to the headteacher, have tea and biscuits and go home well before 9.00 p.m. The biggest decision I sat through as a parent governor pre-LMS was the introduction of a school uniform which required a sub-committee to be set up and a referendum of parents before it was implemented.

Study of the ever-increasing documentation distributed to governors by the then Department of Education and Science (now the Department for Education) and my local authority made clear the extent of the changes facing schools and their governing bodies. We were informed that

> Governors have a general responsibility for the effective management of the school, acting within the framework set by national legislation and by the policies of the LEA [local education authority]. But they are not expected to take detailed decisions about the day to day running of the school – that is the role of the head, whose appointment is one of the most important decisions taken by a governing body. A good head will discuss all main aspects of school life with the governors and expect them to offer general guidance. Since it is for the governors to answer to the parents and the LEA for the running of the school, the head will want to be confident that his actions have their support.
> (*Education (No. 2) Act*, 1986, S32, September 1988a, ch. 3)

All local authorities were required to draw up a scheme for the implementation of LMS in accordance with the requirements of the Education Reform Act of 1988. The scheme for the local management of schools produced by my own local authority reiterated the warning of increased work and responsibilities facing governors:

> Under the scheme the budgets of each primary and secondary school will be determined by means of a formula based on objective assessment of need. Governing bodies will take over management of school budgets Governing bodies will be responsible for the day to day operation of schools, including the appointment of staff, whilst the Authority will remain responsible for determining the total resources available to the school and for strategic policies governing the education service. The Authority will monitor the performance of schools and take remedial action as necessary.
> (Lancashire County Council 1990)

As these two statements became available during my early period as a parent governor, and indeed the second reached me first as a draft for comment from the local authority, I can hardly claim I was not fully informed before I voluntarily took on the role of parent governor. Maybe I should have investigated the legal implications, the committee work, the responsibilities with regard to the appointment of staff in detail, before joining the management team of my daughter's school. In actual fact, back in the mid-1980s and indeed after the introduction of the 1986 Act, this would not have yielded a true insight into what being a school governor now involves.

Perhaps the Secretary of State began to feel a degree of anxiety that governors would immediately resign when they understood the tasks facing them and for that reason, felt obliged to add soothing promises of some sort of philanthropic self-fulfilment in undertaking their greatly increased role:

> At first sight, the range of responsibilities may seem daunting. But governors do not need to be experts in order to tackle them, and may be reassured by the experience of governors of voluntary aided schools, from all walks of life, who have long had the sort of responsibilities county schools will now have.
>   (Introduction, DES, September 1988c)

It is worth pointing out that the reforms contained in the legislation for the introduction of local management of schools were not only financial. One could most certainly be forgiven for thinking that to be the case because of the early emphasis on delegated budgets. Local management of schools was to delegate responsibility across the whole provision of education in schools, and as the Local Management in Schools Initiative claimed, it was to be a

> major management challenge. Management decisions will be required on virtually every aspect of running schools including staff appointments, dismissals, and the marketing of the school to the community.
>   (Local Management in Schools Initiative 1988)

Considering the way in which the changes were spelt out to heads and governors with the emphasis on finance, I am not surprised that it led to the early retirement of many professional and respected headteachers who did not wish to be chief executives or accountants, or to be forced to interact with an often alien technology to run their schools.

1 April 1989 in my local authority marked the beginning of local delegation of finance and all that went with it. The first year served as a pilot, with the budget based on historical costs to allow the LEA to monitor the experience before the introduction of the formal scheme of delegation required by the 1988 Act. Our school was to be fully delegated from 1 April 1990, again as a pilot, rather than as part of a four-year phased introduction as was the case with other schools in the authority.

This early delegation brought a flurry of meetings called by the local authority to explain the scheme and a constant round of meetings of local heads and governors in different schools. Consultation documents and schemes proliferated. The emphasis throughout all the deliberations was on budgets – what was included and what was not; who had responsibility for what and when, and the incessant references to the need to balance budgets within the formula set by the local authority instilled a feeling of dread rather than optimism.

Questions began to be asked about fuel bills and boiler maintenance which had hitherto never even been considered by the governing body. Of major concern was the realization that a cornerstone of the Act was the funding of teachers' salaries at an average rather than an actual level. This had serious implications for our school which had an above average age and long serving staff, but in the early stages of deliberations in our small primary school we could not have imagined just how serious the position would be.

It was at this time that changes began to take place in the composition of our governing body and among our teaching staff. These changes were by no means unique to our school, and I believe reflect the early emphasis on local financial management within LMS. At this stage the teaching staff were too busy dealing with the changes in the National Curriculum to be much involved in management decisions, but the realization was now becoming clear to heads and chairs of governors that they were entering a new era, a market economy for education, and many did not like it. Within a very short space of time our primary school lost its headteacher, deputy headteacher and chair of governors – each with service approaching 20 years. This was no reflection on the head and deputy as teachers, far from it. Rather it showed that they had never seen their chosen career in terms of financial management or accountancy. They were not convinced that the advantages of LMS, namely 'the ability to switch resources as well as the facility, for example to have repairs carried out quickly and efficiently with little administrative fuss' compensated for disadvantages such as:

additional management and administrative tasks which will be required at school level. This may be particularly acute for small primary schools where any flexibility over resource use may be lost in the additional resource costs of meeting the administrative burden. Inevitably there will also be difficulties, especially in the early stages, as schools become accustomed to managing their own affairs to a much greater extent than before.

It is sometimes argued that LMS will interfere with the more traditional duties of headteachers and staff – that of delivering teaching in the classroom. Clearly there is a balance to be struck, but time spent on management is not wasted. The ability to shift resources to match the results of decisions made in the best interests of the school should improve the quality both of learning and of teaching.

(Local Management in Schools Initiative 1988, S1.6)

I have to confess we found it difficult to see the advantages of LMS once we discovered that in our small primary school, the salary costs meant a deficit in our budget which had to be taken from capital – or put another way, from the basic facilities such as the pens, paper and books we were able to provide for the children.

I was elected chair of governors after the then chair resigned to spend more time with her grandchildren. At that stage, we had to face the practical implementation of LMS in the appointment of a new head. Because we were still operating in a transition period for one year before our full delegation, we were fortunate to have considerable professional guidance from our general adviser but even so, we faced a number of difficulties. The *Guide to the Law* produced by the Department of Education and Science (DES) stated quite clearly that the LEA was the actual employer of headteachers and their staff, but that the governors had extensive powers over staffing:

> The head is the key figure in the school. The position must be advertised throughout England and Wales. The governing body will set up the selection panel. This function may not be delegated to a committee. The Chief Education Officer or a representative has a right to attend relevant meetings of the selection panel to offer professional advice but only governors on the selection panel can vote. The governing body has a duty to consider the Chief Education Officer's advice before making a decision. The decision of the selection panel must be endorsed by the full governing body. If there is no decision the governing body has to readvertise the post. The LEA has to appoint the candidate recommended by the governing body unless he or she fails to meet legal requirements on qualifications or health, or is barred from teaching.
>
> (DES 1988c, ch. 10)

In the event the appointment of our new head was far from a fulfilling management experience. Instead it fell some way between a professional appointment and a political circus. The governors were involved at every stage, and the LEA representatives were invaluable in their advice and practical support. However, the influence of the local political authority was inhibiting and although the governors had been ready to shortlist for some time, we had to wait for local councillors to be available to be at the meeting. Because of this we were unable to appoint a new head until the following term so that the deputy had to step in as acting head for the interim period. When the interviews finally took place it was a locally elected member who chaired the panel. We were informed that the delays caused by the involvement of local councillors would not recur once the school had fully delegated status. Even so, the difficulties over the appointment of a new headteacher caused all members of the governing body periods of intense frustration. In addition, the lack of clearly developed LMS policy at that time produced an added burden on the deputy head, all the staff, teaching and non-teaching, and myself as chair of governors. It also coincided with a fairly intense period of the introduction of delegated budgets, particularly with regard to administration through computer networks in the school so that the additional burden on the school clerk and myself was immense. As the final curtain came down on the end-of-term nativity play that year, my thanks to staff, parents and children were particularly warm and heartfelt. I could not say the same about my feelings towards the implementation of LMS.

Eventually a head was appointed. As soon as he took up his post, the deputy head applied for and was granted early retirement. The appointments process started again, but this time without the political representatives. This enabled the head and governors, supported by sound professional guidance from our general adviser, to use the delegated powers to the full and to move quickly to advertise the vacancy.

Looking back at the turbulent times the schools and its governors had to face, I am surprised that staff managed to carry out their professional duties much as before. The school had a staff who had been in post for many years, a head who had taken up post when the school was opened some 20 years earlier, and a head of infants who acted as deputy. Most members of the governing body were long-serving eminent local people, political and non-political representatives of the village community, and the school had the reputation of providing a good family environment which supported the all-round development of the children.

Now within the space of three years, it had lost the head, the deputy, a senior teacher who resigned because of ill health and the chair of governors. A new governing body had taken office which had more parent governor representation. While latter events may have led me to wonder at the teachers' lack of interest in and knowledge about LMS, I wonder now if it was not a necessary protective mechanism to allow personal survival. It was without doubt a busy time for me as chair of governors and there were signs of growing demands on the time of the whole group, but we were still unprepared for the next series of events which were the direct result of the formula funding.

It became necessary to appoint a new member of staff to take the place of the teacher who had resigned because of ill health, and eventually we decided to appoint a mature and experienced teacher. We did consider making a younger and therefore a cheaper appointment, but the mature applicant was clearly the best person for the job. Then our numbers began to fall, as they did in the other primary school in the village. The cost of housing meant fewer young people (and therefore children) in the village, but as the number of children on roll fell, so did our budget. The number was not great, but a loss of five or six children in a small primary school when salary costs are already greater than income, is sufficient to cause problems.

Since the introduction of LMS, our governing body had been concerned to the point of obsession at times with the funding allocation for teachers' salaries. The manifestation in our budget of average as opposed to actual salary costs gave us a deficit in the region of £5000. Now, with a falling roll, we needed to review the staffing requirements. Members of staff of the school had been a tower of strength during all the changes, but now it was their turn to be part of what the LMS Guide described as 'the flexibility and choice that LMS engenders'. The teachers now became part of the financial formula and the employment of teachers, or not, appeared to be the only way out of our funding problems as we had nothing left to cut.

We had one member of staff on a permanent half-time contract and one temporary half-time teacher whose contract we thought we could review each year within our staffing powers. It seemed to us that the only way we could save money was to dispense with the services of the temporary teacher. We looked to the DES *Guide to the Law* for guidance about the legal position relating to the employment of teachers. Section 11 states that:

> If the school has a delegated budget, the LEA cannot lay down a staffing complement for it. When a member of staff leaves it will be for the governors to decide whether he is to be replaced. The LEA may give advice on the number and mix of staff that would be consistent with the school's budget and delivery of the curriculum. The governing body will want to take this advice carefully into account when considering appointments.

And Section 14 makes clear that:

If the governors are managing a delegated budget as part of a scheme of financial delegation, they have extensive powers over staffing. Decisions about staffing are both important and complex, and governing bodies will want to ensure that they make full use of all the sources of advice available to them.

It was not until 1993 that we were reminded that in spite of our 'extensive staffing powers', we had responsibilities under employment law (DFE 1993).

We decided to seek advice as suggested in the *Guide to Law* and went with confidence to the LEA staffing personnel section, as the LEA is in fact the employer of staff. As a governing body, we were becoming increasingly uneasy in our role. We knew the local authority had a 'no redundancy' policy but we also knew we were running into deficit. It was significant to me that different governors approached the situation in different ways. To the business orientated members, there was no problem. We should decide not to renew the contract of the part-time temporary member of staff to make immediate savings. As chair of governors, a parent and an ex-teacher, I felt a great concern for the actual individual involved and the implications for the school of the loss of her professional expertise. The teachers raised the question of professional support and loyalty towards long-serving colleagues. The advice from the local authority staffing section was that we had the power to terminate the contract which the part-time teacher had had for five years and that her departure would then allow us to consider some reorganization in the school.

Once this was announced, the part-time teacher took legal advice from her Union. Owing to the length of time she had been employed in the school and the number of hours she worked each week, we discovered we could *not* terminate her employment. Not only did we not have the authority within employment legislation, but it was also stated that we should not have put her under the stress of having singled her out as a possible solution to the budget problem. We had for some time been concerned about our own legal position. We were fortunate to have a co-opted parent governor who was a solicitor and he attempted with little success to clarify the limit of our liability. The LEA, when pressed, pointed to a catch-all phrase which indicated that 'governors will not incur any personal liability in respect of the exercise of their powers under the scheme (LMS), provided they had acted in good faith'. We had acted in good faith and with the full advice of the local authority, but we still found ourselves in the position of facing possible legal action. Our solicitor would have been unable to practise if he had legal action pending against him and other governors had similar worries about the limits of their financial liabilities if action for compensation for unfair dismissal was taken against them. The position looked grim for the whole governing body.

What followed is too long and complex to relate here, but illustrates the worst possible scenario for a chair of governors. We were back facing the same budget problems with no quick solution and a possible legal action pending.

Our general adviser, the Chief Staffing Officer, and the Area Team Leader (the LEA administrator in charge of our district), all visited the school and confirmed they had given wrong advice. We tried to enlist the help of the governor training section for definitive interpretation of the law relating to the employment of staff, but to no avail. We invited the local Member of Parliament to visit us who was unhelpful and made suggestions which demonstrated a total lack of understanding of LMS issues – even at one stage suggesting I might think about having more children to boost school numbers!

Governors' meetings now took on a new emphasis as we had to reconsider all previous and any new options. We had meetings with all the teaching and non-teaching staff and with LEA senior officials. I met with staff, and every possible option for reducing our staff complement was considered. All the scenarios under the LEA scheme were pointed out. Nothing was said to me in the meeting, but an official complaint came back that I had looked at one person and so put undue pressure on her. This alone gives an indication of how bad things were for us all. The head and I saw each of the staff individually to discuss options and to ask if they had solutions. No one had, and as all jobs were now seen to be equally vulnerable, it is little wonder no-one wanted to be part of a decision.

Shortly before the end of term one of our longest serving staff members decided in the light of the offers made to her by the authority that she would take early retirement. It was pointed out that she would be unlikely to get such a good deal again, and although it was earlier than she would have liked, she decided to go.

Our financial problems were partly solved to the extent that we were then able to offer a permanent full-time appointment to the temporary part-time teacher, provided the head taught part-time in future in the split class.

On the last day of term a white-faced group of teachers left the school for the summer break. The governors, however, gathered for a meeting after school. When I first became a parent governor, we had three meetings each year. This was the thirteenth meeting of the year, many having lasted until after 11.00 p.m. or later.

It seemed that there was going to be no action taken against us as a governing body, but our members wanted our position to be clarified once and for all. The LEA had throughout not made us feel secure about how far we would be supported in case of legal action, and our solicitor member wanted a statement in writing. He drafted a letter which was faxed to me while I was working in a different part of the county. I forwarded it to the Chief Education Officer and asked him to confirm the limits of our responsibility in future.

I think what was highlighted to my governing body by this scenario, was the way in which the implications of the introduction of a scheme as far-reaching as LMS had been implemented without careful consideration of the practical consequences. Since the time we now refer to as the terrible year in school, we have been able to become more aware of what I see as the stated advantages of LMS, and because governors were able to make out a case for funding from the local authority's contingency fund, our budget is temporarily sound. After a difficult year when our school clerk resigned due to a stress-related illness, and our head also began to show symptoms of stress and had to reassess his role, we began a period of consolidation and constructive development. We have made some important staffing decisions within our budget which will benefit the children and support all the staff, and I feel optimistic that staff and governors are working together in harmony again. We recently held a training day for staff and governors with an educational management consultant looking at our roles as they contribute to the school as a whole. It was a worthwhile and challenging day with positive outcomes.

Complacency cannot set in though. Our real staff costs are eating away the small surplus from the contingency. We are now very wary of any decision we make about anything, and spend time pouring over handbooks to cover all legal liabilities. We are certainly well known in the authority for the learning experiences we had (and which we do not intend to repeat) and from the opportunities we gave to the LEA to tighten up procedures without having to become involved in any real legal situations. We have recently found that our committee structure in the school may not stand up to a tribunal investigation if any case came to court, so we are to hold a special meeting to make sure all is well before our inspection by the Office for Standards in Education (OFSTED). The inspection will be another hurdle to face as the chair of governors again plays a large unpaid and responsible role, and teachers again find themselves under investigation. However, just as it may seem possible to look towards any advantages of local financial management in schools our position with regard to funding staff salaries looks as if it will become critical again. We currently await the decision about the amount which will be added to our budget to fund the latest teacher pay increase of 2.9 per cent. Rumour has it that this may be as much as 1.5 per cent, but on our already increasing deficit, the difference will be impossible to cover. Added to that, I have recently received notification from the Secretary of State that the governors must now make an annual review of the performance and salaries of the head and deputy head. As there is little money for paper and pencils, the head, who has not had an increase in salary since he took up post, feels that he cannot make a claim against a budget already about to go into deficit.

As I consider the problems facing my particular small primary school, I read of others who, in a similar position, can only resolve the difficulties by appointing temporary staff on short-term contracts. The career prospects for teachers seem to be little longer than three years before they then become too expensive. A recent request to the Department for Education to review the formula funding for primary schools particularly to consider the age weighting of top juniors and lower secondary brought no change, but then it would not have been likely considering the large number of requests which came from primary heads and governors.

The implications for teachers under LMS are apparent for all to see. I can only hope that we can find a solution through a closer working relationship with teachers, who are after all the professionals, which will again allow us to focus on children in schools – though in the meantime I strive to solve my latest budget crisis.

Part four

SUBJECT TO CHANGE

11

CAREERS EDUCATION:

THE FIGHT FOR

RECOGNITION

Lorna Unwin

Introduction

Careers education has, in the majority of schools, traditionally had
to be grateful for a relatively small amount of lesson space and
careers education teachers have had to fight their corner against the
more powerful timetable demands of their subject based colleagues
(see Harris 1992). As it is not bound by examination pressures in
terms of content or regulations, the pattern of careers education
differs enormously from school to school. Time for careers education has been allocated during form periods at the start of the day,
in short lessons under the more general banner of personal and
social education (PSE), or restricted to talks for older pupils by invited speakers. In some schools, careers education touches all age
groups, whereas in others it does not appear on timetables until
Year 10 (14/15 year-olds). This *ad hoc* approach to careers education
provision has not been helped by the National Curriculum which
gives careers education provision the ambiguous classification of a
cross-curricular theme, along with economic and industrial understanding, education for citizenship, health education and environ-
mental education. As Watts has pointed out, these cross-curricular

themes have received little attention from the official bodies responsible for overseeing the National Curriculum or from the Dearing Report (Watts 1994). Nevertheless, the former National Curriculum Council in its guidelines for careers education clearly expected a great deal from schools:

> Much careers education and guidance can be provided within the subjects of the National Curriculum and other elements of the whole curriculum, and will be the responsibility of all teachers. It will also involve a range of adults who are able to provide direct experience of work and links with the community outside school. Other aspects may require separate and specialist provision, especially in Years 10 and 11 where pupils will also need individual careers guidance. This is best offered by careers officers working with trained careers teachers/co-ordinators and with group or form tutors.
>
> (NCC 1990)

The ambiguity surrounding careers education is matched by confusion and concern about the future shape and control of careers guidance as delivered by the Careers Service. In 1995, the Careers Service at local level will be effectively up for tender. In 1994, local Careers Services were taken out of local education authority (LEA) control and placed in a temporary 'partnership' with Training and Enterprise Councils (TECs). In 1995, the Department of Employment (DE) will invite bids from organizations (including the careers services themselves) to deliver careers guidance in schools and colleges. The uncertainty about what kind of careers service will emerge from this restructuring will put more pressure on careers education teachers to ensure that young people acquire an adequate understanding of their post-16 options.

This chapter explores the paradoxical situation in which careers education struggles to survive at a time when its usefulness has never been more appropriate. Part of the chapter draws on the experiences of the head of careers at Knutsford High School who serves as an illustration of the creativity and enormous effort required if schools are to provide their young people with an effective careers education and guidance service.

Making choices in a changing world

The context for the chapter is the challenge facing schools and the country as a whole to improve the curriculum menu for the majority of young people who do not progress along a traditional academic route and aspire to enter higher education. In addition, the changing nature of the labour market and the fact that, for some years, young people have no longer been able to walk straight into employment after leaving school, have increased the need for more substantial careers education. A careers officer in a Year 11 guidance interview with 16 year-old pupils, has to cover a plethora of routes including school sixth form, full-time and part-time further education, government-sponsored training schemes, employment with day-release training, employment without training and unemployment, as well as giving advice about standard job vacancies. Careers education can no longer rely on the services of a few local people – police officers, bank managers, nurses – coming in to school to talk about their particular career routes.

Against this background, the Department for Education (DFE), and the DE, sometimes working together, sometimes not, have promoted four initiatives which seek to prepare young people for their life beyond school:

1 Records of Achievement (ROAs);
2 Careers Action Planning;
3 Youth Credits (introduced as Training Credits in 1990 but changed to Youth Credits in 1993);
4 Work Experience.

Three of the initiatives – ROAs, action planning and work experience – developed out of the Technical and Vocational Education Initiative (TVEI). Youth Credits is a DE initiative which is being phased in throughout England, Wales and Scotland to replace current Youth Training (YT) arrangements. The government intends that, by 1996, every 16–18 year-old who wishes to leave full-time education will do so holding a Youth Credit which they can trade in for a minimum of two years' vocational training (see Unwin 1993). All four initiatives require time to be set aside within an already crowded school day in order that pupils participate in related activities and obtain information. In the case of the statutory work experience programme, pupils in Years 10 and 11 must spend two weeks out of school in a work setting. Central to the success and long-term development of these initiatives are those teachers with specific responsibility for careers education.

Careers education teachers have, for a long time, worked with their colleagues in the careers service, but since 1990 they have been increasingly involved with a new set of colleagues, the staff of their local TEC. (The TEC equivalent in Scotland is a Local Enterprise Company (LEC).) Both Youth Credits and Action Planning are controlled and driven by TECs who are also involved, along with LEAs, with the development of ROAs and the organization of the work experience programme. The TECs represent a potential new source of money for schools, but, as importantly, a source of much needed expertise and information about the world of vocational education and training beyond school.

In many areas, this relationship between schools and TECs operates within a formally established education–business partnership (EBP). The following section of this chapter examines the work of the head of careers education at Knutsford High School, which is a member of an EBP managed by South and East Cheshire TEC.

Careers education in Knutsford: a whole-school approach

Knutsford High School is a large 11–18 comprehensive school situated in a prosperous Cheshire market town within commuting distance of the Greater Manchester conurbation. Pupils at the school come from a wide range of backgrounds and the school's academic results place it high in both county and national league tables. As a member of the South and East Cheshire EBP, the school has, since 1991, received grants totalling £5000 to upgrade its careers resources room which is available to all pupils from Year 9 onwards. The room, which contains a variety of multi-media information about post-16 routes, is open all day from as early as 8.00 a.m. and does not close until the careers teachers leave the building, often as late as 5.30 p.m.

The school's policy statement for careers education states:

Careers education and guidance should provide all young people with the skills, knowledge and information to enable them to make considered educational and careers decisions, which are consistent with their abilities and needs, in the context of a complex and changing world.

This statement is then broken down into the following purposes:

1 To help individuals to become aware of themselves, their skills, abilities, interests and values.
2 To encourage interest in, and awareness of, the widest range of opportunities available in education, training and employment.
3 To develop skills required to make informed, reasoned decisions.
4 To develop skills needed in coping with significant changes in their lives. Careers education should, therefore, aim to help students to make informed choices about their futures,

to implement their decisions and to create longer-term plans for progression.

In order to achieve its aims, the school has adopted a whole-school approach to careers education and guidance. It is worth describing the elements of this approach as they indicate the complex organization required to sustain an ambitious programme.

Careers education begins in Year 7 (first secondary year) at Knutsford with a programme which focuses on the development of 'self-worth, personal and social skills, particularly communications skills and group skills'. In Years 7 and 8, this programme forms part of the pastoral element of school life and involves other curriculum subjects as appropriate. In Years 9, 10 and 11, careers education is delivered through PSE, pastoral activities and curriculum subjects. The work experience programme takes place in Year 10, prior to which pupils explore their ideas about the preferences for their future careers by taking part in the Job Ideas and Information Generator – Computer Assisted Learning (JIIG–CAL). Careers action planning also begins in Year 10, building on the pupils' ROAs which they begin compiling in Year 7. Action Planning involves the local careers officers who see every pupil for at least one personal guidance interview, and continues into Year 11 when pupils also receive information about Youth Credits. For those who stay at the school after 16, there are opportunities to review and update action plans throughout Years 12 and 13, and those pupils who pursue vocational education courses can spend up to three weeks in Year 12 in a work placement related to their course. Indeed, the growth of the one-year sixth form has meant that the careers team has to ensure that pupils planning to leave full-time education at 17 receive adequate guidance and review the plans they made at 16.

As part of the Youth Credits initiative managed by South and East Cheshire TEC, young people who choose to stay in full-time education whether at school or college, can apply for individual awards to finance personal development projects, for example: work experience abroad to improve language skills; field work for an A Level subject; attending an assertiveness course. Like the other schools in the area, Knutsford is allocated an annual pot of money for the awards and encourages sixth formers to make a case for funding.

Back in the mid-1970s when Anne Rowlands, Knutsford's current head of careers education and PSE, became involved with careers teaching at the school, the picture was very different. She recalled that:

it seemed very basic then. I arranged interviews for pupils in Year 11 with the Careers Officer and liaised with subject teachers

so that pupils could be withdrawn from lessons. There was
nothing in the way of careers education for sixth formers.

Anne believes the first major boost for careers education came
with the introduction, through TVEI, of the work experience programme which involved the school directly with local employers.
In addition, the school had to persuade parents that it would be
beneficial for their children to spend time away from school, thus
highlighting the important role of careers education in the curriculum. The second important innovation was the introduction of
JIIG–CAL, again funded under TVEI. JIIG–CAL enables pupils to explore their careers ideas in depth, producing printed analyses which
they can discuss with teachers, careers officers and parents. Careers
action planning has also proved to be very useful as it has enabled
careers officers to spend more time in the school and work with
pupils at both an earlier and later stage. A central feature of JIIG–
CAL, action planning, work experience and ROAs, is that they all
demand well-organized, formal recording systems so that all the
activities are interrelated. Anne commented that these initiatives
have raised the profile of careers education by giving it a much more
professional appearance and feel. The subject teachers in the school
have seen the value of doing the job of careers education properly.
They see pupils motivated by the JIIG–CAL exercises, and this gets
transferred into the different subject areas.
    She is quick to point out, however, that careers education teachers
cannot afford to be complacent as the conflicting demands made on
the curriculum and teachers' time are increasing. She believes that
Knutsford has made enormous strides forward by having a careers
education policy which is fully supported by the headteacher and
senior management team. This has enabled her to create a specialist
team, based in one office, which spans careers education, PSE, and
the school's pastoral programme. The team comprises a vocational
tutor responsible for organizing work experience, a pre-vocational
tutor who is co-ordinating the introduction of General National
Vocational Qualifications (GNVQs) into the school, and Anne herself.
All three also teach in the mainstream curriculum. Anne, for example,
teaches science and geography for 29 lessons out of a 50-lesson, 10-
day timetable.
    In order to maintain this integrated approach, Anne's team has
to work closely with pupils in every year of the school. Her main
vehicle for this is through the team's responsibility for co-ordinating
input about careers education and PSE-related topics in the tutor
period held at the start of each day. This also enables the team to
keep directly in touch with subject teachers. Further involvement

with subject teachers comes through their responsibilities related to completion of ROAs and through specialist activities. One such activity, for example, linked the geography department with a local company resulting in the creation of a curriculum project.

The most significant way in which her senior colleagues can support careers education is through the allocation of time and resources. All Knutsford pupils take part in PSE lessons, which encompass careers education for 55 minutes every alternate week. In Year 9, this is increased by a further hour a week and in Year 10, pupils have three PSE sessions every 10 days. PSE time allocated in Years 12 and 13, forms the core of the General Studies curriculum. Modest, but important increases in time have been made over the 18 years that Anne has been involved, and she is hopeful that even more space may be found on the timetable. For Anne, this has meant a continued struggle to keep the spotlight on her area:

Careers education has to fight its corner. That means you have to be committed to convince your colleagues that it is as important to pupils as any other subject. It would be very easy for careers education to get diluted so my colleagues and I have to show constant enthusiasm. The pupils certainly show it – our resources room is always busy with pupils working at the computer terminals, borrowing careers videos, sitting discussing ideas and so on.

Meetings, meetings, meetings

If Anne and her team are busy during the normal school day, they work equally as hard outside the official school hours. The biggest demand on their time comes from attending meetings called by the range of organizations which bring together the different sectors of the local community. They include:

1 Education–Business Partnership (monthly meeting);
2 South and East Cheshire TEC;
3 Wilmslow/Knutsford Crime Prevention Panel (monthly meeting);
4 Rotary and Lions Clubs (usually monthly meetings);
5 Macclesfield Health Authority – Health Promotion Unit.

Anne commented that these organizations supplied her team with information, contacts, and ideas. The Crime Prevention Panel, for example, provided material for PSE lessons, possible sources of funding for student projects and, through links with employers on the panel, offers of placements for the work experience programme. In addition to these community groups, the careers team also attend meetings of the Macclesfield Careers Teachers' group to share experiences and develop new approaches.

On an individual basis, the school has direct contact with a number of employers including two multinational companies based near to the school. Anne liaises on a regular basis with these employers who come and speak to pupils, organize competitions, invite pupils to visit their premises and generally play a part in the life of the school. She commented:

> As a careers teacher, you have to be able and willing to mix with an enormous range of people – managing directors, chief constables, personnel officers, production managers, newspaper editors and reporters and so on. I just see it as part of my job. All these people are useful to me and the school, and talking to them keeps me in touch with the world our pupils will be entering. They are also usually incredibly enthusiastic about helping the school – I have to work hard sometimes to keep up with them!

A professional approach

The imposition of competitive league tables and the pressure for all schools to raise the level of their academic achievements, ensures that careers education will have to continue its struggle for recognition and status alongside its more favoured relatives on the timetable. Anne believes that careers education must be seen to be professionally managed in order to gain and keep the respect of teachers and senior management. She feels strongly that:

> this means that senior management must take responsibility for ensuring that careers education is treated seriously. It needs real time allocated to it. It needs to be organised by a specialist team with access to a secretary and office space for all the paperwork. It needs well trained staff who keep themselves up to date by attending courses organised by the Careers Service, the local TEC and other organisations.

Perhaps even more important is the need for

> government to promote the use of records of achievement and action plans with employers. It should also strengthen its commitment to cross-curricular themes in the National Curriculum.

Conclusion

The work of careers teachers deserves far greater attention. Despite calls by the 'great and the good' including the Confederation of British Industry and the Trades Union Congress for careers education and guidance to be given increased status and resources, it is still down to individual teachers like those at Knutsford to fight the battle. That they do so at the same time as carrying out their duties as subject teachers is remarkable. Anne summed up her feelings thus:

> It's hard work, especially when I have to race from school to an early evening meeting and then get home to start marking and preparation. I do feel a great sense of satisfaction though when we have visitors to the school as they usually ask to see the careers resources centre – then I feel appreciated. The biggest buzz, though, comes from the pupils who have a real thirst for knowledge about the world of work, and who really enjoy exploring the possibilities. I still think I've got a lot to learn about the area. I never stop thinking I could do this in a better way.

Acknowledgements

This chapter could not have been written without the assistance and encouragement of Anne Rowlands, head of careers education at Knutsford High School and the co-operation of the school's headteacher, Michael Valleley. I would also like to thank staff of Cheshire's Careers Service and South and East Cheshire TEC for their assistance.

12

AT THE CORE:

'OH, TO BE IN ENGLAND'

Stephen Waters

Oh, to be in England
Now that April's there...

And after April, when May follows,
And the whitethroat builds, and all the swallows!...
And though the fields look rough with hoary dew,
All will be gay when noontide wakes anew
The buttercups, the little children's dower,
– Far brighter than this gaudy melon-flower!

Robert Browning's poem 'Home-Thoughts, from Abroad' seems an apt starting point for my reflections on the demise of English teaching in the National Curriculum and my account of the struggle, as one English teacher among many, to cope with relentless change. For one thing, Browning's poem appeared in the 1993 Key Stage 3 Anthology which was required reading for Paper 2: Test of Prior Reading in the Standard Assessment Tests (SATs). For another, Browning was writing about the month of April, at the same time of year as I began this chapter. There, however, the similarities end. Whereas Browning was in no doubt about the attractions of his native land, I find it difficult to share his unreserved optimism or sentimental fervour. Indeed, I doubt whether there has been a time since I began teaching in 1976 when the morale of English teachers has been so fiercely undermined and our professional judgement so poorly respected. The story of how we have come to be in this position is indeed a turbulent one.

A personal account always runs the risk of being unrepresentative. For this reason, and because I owe it to the many English teachers who feel as I do today, I have chosen to place my personal reflections in the wider context of the educational policy-making which has had such a devastating impact on English teaching in particular and on the teaching profession in general. From my reading of the educational press, my attendance at conferences and from my conversations with teachers of English, I am confident that my perspective will be shared by many English departments in both state and independent schools.

My teaching experience to date is not untypical. I began teaching in 1976 in an 11–18 mixed comprehensive school in the South West of England some seven years after Brian Cox had published the first of his Black Papers on the teaching of grammar and reading (Cox and Dyson 1969a), and one year after the publication of the Bullock Report (DES 1975), the first of several major inquiries into the teaching of English to have taken place during the last 20 years. After just over two years in my first post, I taught for a further five years in an 11–16 comprehensive school during which time I became head of drama, a subject now threatened by National Curriculum timetable constraints and given little recognition in the proposed Revised Orders for English. Since 1984, I have taught in an 11–18 school in the North of England and currently hold a responsibility post as Second in Department with specific responsibility for English at Key Stage 3. Over the course of the last 10 years I have seen the English curriculum alter beyond recognition; my professional autonomy severely curtailed; and my department subjected to unprecedented change as the government has taken an increasingly centralist role in curriculum content and assessment.

When I first began teaching the classroom was the English teacher's domain and, although often vigorously and publicly debated, English as a subject was largely under the control of the class teacher who operated within a departmental framework. Course content, teaching methodology and assessment procedures were informed by a combination: of advice from the then Department of Education and Science (DES); local education authority (LEA) policy; and good practice disseminated and encouraged by organizations like the National Association for the Teaching of English (NATE). In many departments – including the one in which I then taught – a combination of traditional and progressive teaching took place. Contrary to the frequent assertions of the media that there was a lack of structured teaching and an over-emphasis on creativity at the expense of technical accuracy, we were anxious to get the balance right. Little changed in English teaching practice, despite Prime Minister Callaghan's famous Ruskin College speech in 1976, until the mid-1980s, around the time when I took up my appointment in my present school. Since then an English national curriculum has been imposed; an assessment procedure based on a 10-level grading system put in place; GCSE introduced and of late subjected to a course work limit of 40 per cent; a major inquiry set up into the teaching of English (the Kingman Inquiry); a massive in-service programme initiated to train teachers more effectively to teach English language; a revision of the English National Curriculum proposed only four years after it was first implemented; and, more recently, through the Dearing Report, a major review of the entire National Curriculum and its assessment procedures.

Where are we now?

The status quo, as it was when I began to write in April 1993, altered considerably by the time the chapter was completed in February 1994. During the first three months of 1993 there had been unprecedented media coverage of English and its place in the National Curriculum, mainly focusing on the assessment of English through the Key Stage 3 SATs. There was also anger and dismay, not only confined to the state sector, that a revision of the English National Curriculum Order was in progress, following the National Curriculum Council's (NCC) report on the matter in 1992. The Headmaster's Conference had already advised its members not to participate in National Curriculum testing and was quoted in *The Times Educational Supplement* (8 January 1993) as saying: 'I don't think the boycott should be seen as a political union statement – this goes far wider than union action.'

Joan Clanchy, Head of North London Collegiate School – an independent girls' school – resigned in February from the NCC in protest at the imminent amendment to the English curriculum because: 'the dominant aim has become a curriculum designed for tests and the result is a model which is barren and anti-intellectual' (*The Times Educational Supplement*, 5 March 1993).

Three days after Joan Cianchy's statement, the National Association of Schoolmasters/Union of Women Teachers announced a boycott of all National Curriculum assessment, the ballot having been prompted initially by the dissatisfaction of English teachers. During the summer term, the opposition to John Patten, the Secretary of State for Education, was to intensify. The Association of Teachers and Lecturers and then the National Union of Teachers voted over-whelmingly to join the boycott, effectively putting an end to the wholesale testing of pupils in 1993. At the same time, parents' groups, including the National Confederation of Parent–Teacher Associations, were asking for the SATs to be made voluntary. By June, the National Association of Headteachers was calling for the suspension of school league tables which were to have been published along with the SATs results.

It would be impossible to find a parallel situation in education in which so many interest groups, including the private sector, had so much in common and were so firmly united against government policy. If the English SATs had triggered the wave of anger, it was the arrival of the Revised English Order for consultation in schools at the end of May which was to be the final straw. The news of the revision had prompted Brian Cox, who had chaired the original English National Curriculum working group, to speak out in public against it. One of his most outspoken attacks came in the Channel 4 television programme 'Opinions', broadcast on 28 February 1993 which appeared as a transcript in *The Times* newspaper on the following day. Referring to his contribution to the Black Papers in 1969, Professor Cox claimed that he had been consistent in his views on English teaching – what had changed significantly was the ideological background against which his remarks were being judged. His analysis of the government's intentions towards the English curriculum was politically blunt:

> The right-wingers are attacking the present curriculum because they want to preserve a unity and stability based on the hegemony imposed by the upper and middle classes in the 1930s and before. The texts they prescribe often seem more suited to the days of British imperialism.
>
> (*The Times*, 1 March 1993)

Indeed, Robert Browning could easily have been one of the authors Cox had in mind when he attacked the literature selected for the proposed revision to the English National Curriculum. The selection was heavily influenced by what Cox had called the 'cultural heritage' view of English in his original Working Group submission 'English for ages 5 to 16' (commonly known as the Cox Report, DES 1989a). Cox had defined this view as 'an appreciation of those works of literature that have been widely regarded as amongst the finest in the language' (para. 2.24). What was dangerous about the new proposals, Cox argued, was that the cultural heritage model of literature was being allowed to dominate the curriculum to the exclusion of other views which, in embracing both personal response and cultural analysis, led pupils towards an understanding of the context within which literature was written and an examination of the values expressed by it. Cox's criticism was well-founded; the selection of literature at Key Stages 3 and 4 specified the inclusion of a number of texts written before 1900. This view of literature as informed by works known in popular parlance as 'classics' presupposed that society was mono-lingual, class-based and uninfluenced by groups other than those belonging to the dominant culture. As Rebecca Bunting put it:

> Novels and poems in this category are treated as repositories of all that we value in our culture, and to read them is to expose ourselves to their effects. Central to these is the desire to bind a nation together through a common literary heritage, to buff down the hard edges of pluralism and bring us all together, in strength, through the harmonising forces of good literature. Once achieved, the nation will be stronger and levels of literacy will rise because standards will improve . . . The process of reading becomes a passive activity for readers, who have no option but to allow themselves to be bathed in the writer's intentions, and who must be open to the moral influence of the classics.
>
> (Bunting 1993: 3)

The society which was envisaged by the new English curriculum was not one which would be easily recognized by English teachers in their classrooms.

Cox was rightly concerned that the National Curriculum in English, which teachers had struggled to deliver and assess against overwhelming odds, was being manipulated by a government who understood little about language development or the complexity of the relationship between the teacher, the pupil, and the reading and writing process. Concern about the government's interpretation of that relationship was also at the centre of the objections to the SATs which were, according to Lord Griffiths of Fforestfach, then Chair of the Schools Examination and Assessment Council, innocuously designed to provide 'a snapshot of pupils' attainment at a particular time' (*The Times Educational Supplement*, 29 January 1993). The full story of the English SATs merits detailed coverage; space dictates, however, that only key events can be highlighted here.

On 15 January 1993, Peter Harding, head of English at Carre's Grammar School in Sleaford, wrote to *The Times Educational Supplement* to explain why he could no longer be a member of the School Examinations and Assessment Council (SEAC) English committee, headed by John Marenbon, director of English Studies at

Trinity College, Cambridge and an expert in medieval philosophy. Harding recounted how there had been no consultation over the Key Stage 3 anthology set for SAT Paper 2: Test of Prior Reading, and expressed his general concern at both the format of the tests and the fact that a pilot of the sample SATs papers had been conducted in secrecy with older pupils in only a small number of schools. Two weeks later, the papers were leaked to the National Union of Teachers and to several newspapers, including *The Times Educational Supplement*. There was a great deal of speculation that the government had used 'live' questions, intending that the tests would not be altered whatever the outcome of the pilot. In any event, the leak forced SEAC to prepare a new batch of test papers.

Peter Harding was right; the anthology was a curious mixture of extracts which seem to have been chosen not so much because they were intrinsically fascinating but because those responsible for their selection seemed to feel that it would do pupils good to be exposed to worthy works of literature in the cultural heritage tradition, no matter how lacking in relevance or unimaginative in content. There was, for example, an abridged extract of *David Copperfield*; William Wordsworth's 'The Daffodils' printed opposite an extract from Dorothy Wordsworth's diary; a section from Chaucer's Prologue to *The Canterbury Tales* in both the original and in translation; 'Home-Thoughts, from Abroad', the Browning poem which opened this chapter; and – reputedly chosen by Marenbon himself – an extract from 'Rasselas' by Samuel Johnson.

If the anthology was, in the words of Peter Harding, 'dull', 'uninspiring' and 'alien', the remainder of the SAT reading paper was reactionary and divisive. Although the SATs ensured that Shakespeare was read at Key Stage 3, only those deemed to be at Level 5 or above were allowed to answer questions on one of the three plays selected. Levels 3–4 would be tested instead on a text chosen from a specified list by the class teacher. Presumably in the interests of academic rigour, pupils on Level 5 and above would not be allowed to consult their text, the Shakespeare play, during the test; pupils on Levels 3 and 4, on the other hand, could answer questions in open-text conditions. The type of questions which were set on the Shakespeare section of the sample paper took me back to the days of the General Certificate of Education (GCE), O Level English Literature examinations when candidates were given context questions which emphasized the search for meaning rather than the expression of literary appreciation. It was clear that, as one of the aims of the SATs was to provide a standardized assessment of each pupil's progress, predetermined answers according to a structured mark scheme were to be demanded and, in marking the candidates' answers, teachers were to be allowed little opportunity to exercise discretion for creative responses.

Other aspects of the SATs were equally worrying. For example, there was the section on 'Use of Language' in Test 1: Test of Reading and Writing. According to the advice given in the SEAC School Assessment Folder 'Information on the 1993 Tests', candidates would be required to read two passages, provide alternative words or phrases to words selected from the first passage and complete a cloze exercise on the second. Page 14 of the booklet explained the aim of this section of the paper like this:

> Questions on the first of these passages allow pupils to demonstrate the ability to make appropriate lexical choices; those on the second passage test the appropriate use of grammar. *They are not reading comprehension exercises.* (My italics)

How could such an exercise fail but to be a test of reading understanding? The ability to 'make appropriate lexical choices' depended on the pupil grasping the meanings of words or phrases as they were used in the context of the passage. What was possibly meant was that this part of the test would be marked in such a way as to reflect assessment of Attainment Target 2: Writing. Whatever the intention, this example at best demonstrated the illogicality of attempting to test each attainment target as a separate skill and at worst reflected an incomplete understanding of the interdependence between knowledge about language and reading ability.

There was also the extended writing task on Paper 3 which would, the booklet optimistically and perhaps disingenuously asserted, in the hour allowed provide 'opportunities for pupils to plan and revise their work'! If this advice was intended to be taken seriously, it was no more than a token gesture to the vital work English teachers were carrying out with pupils on drafting and re-drafting writing in the classroom.

There was so much in the tests that seemed to relegate English to the days when the quality of written response and the depth of literary understanding were measured by what could be learnt or predicted in advance and regurgitated at the appropriate moment. There was so much that jarred with, and even contradicted, the National Curriculum itself that I became angry and perplexed in equal measure at how I was to steer the department towards preparing pupils for these ill-conceived tests. John Denham, head of English at King Edward V1 Camp Hill School for Boys, Birmingham, did not over-state the case when he described the SATs as bringing about

hopeless confusion and [an] immense burden of unproductive
administration which is engulfing us and threatening to destroy
the pleasure of giving and receiving education.

(The Times Educational Supplement, 29 January 1993)

We decided to make sense out of the confusion surrounding the
National Curriculum SATs by tackling the issue of the tiers of entry
to the reading paper. The department took the view that it would
be divisive and contrary to the spirit of the National Curriculum to
teach Shakespeare only to pupils of Level 5 and above. We would,
therefore, continue to teach pupils in mixed ability groups and offer
everyone 'Romeo and Juliet' or 'A Midsummer Night's Dream' and
one of the texts from the prescribed list for Levels 3 and 4. Course
work would be set on both the Shakespeare play and the Level 3–
4 text and the writing produced would contribute to each pupil's
English folder. Avoiding grouping pupils in specific tiers would enable
us to postpone their allocation to a particular level which would in
turn determine their tier of entry to the SATs. We also decided to
produce an in-house pupil booklet to guide our pupils through the
anthology. We felt that it would be counter-productive to class-
teach each of the required texts and judged that we could encourage
imaginative course work on each of the texts if pupils worked through
them at their own speed, with the booklet beside them for assistance and their teacher to advise them when necessary.

As the SATs did not take place, the success of our approach has
never been fully evaluated. We believe, however, that the benefits of
teaching all pupils the same curriculum and resisting the government's intention that only those of above-average ability would
study Shakespeare outweighed the difficulties of segregating pupils
in the way the tests presupposed. Whatever the outcome would
have been, we felt at the time that, given the circumstances, this
was the compromise which allowed us to exercise our professional
judgement and to create the most educationally acceptable alternative
to the Year 9 curriculum and assessment process.

Imagine the position of my own department in March 1993. We
had undertaken extensive preparation of resources to enable us to
deliver the National Curriculum as effectively as possible during the
course of the previous three years, including the production of units
of work linked to the programmes of study, and modules enabling
all pupils to study a Shakespeare text in mixed ability groups; we
had examined ways of integrating language teaching into our classroom resources, and speaking and listening had been given greater
prominence; we had emphasized drafting to the pupils as a crucial
part of the writing process; and we were moving towards a system

of basing our assessment of levels of attainment on the written evidence collected by pupils in their English folders during Key Stage 3. Like many departments, we were attempting to translate the aims and intentions of the National Curriculum into successful practice.

The government, in its repeated public insistence on the extent to which the National Curriculum had been universally acknowledged and well-received, failed to appreciate what a major organizational change was required in departments like my own to make it work successfully. There was much in the National Curriculum that matched our notion of good practice but there were also serious anomalies, particularly in the assessment process, with which we are still grappling today. Language development, for example, a recursive skill, was measured on the 10-level scale as if it progressed in regular steps. English as a subject was broken up into the separate assessment areas of Speaking and Listening; Reading; and Writing when so much successful teaching avoided such arbitrary distinctions and drew on all three areas simultaneously. Extensive records of pupils' progress in the statements of attainment were meant to be kept in such a way that it would have turned us into clip-board monitors had we attempted to fulfil the law to the letter. We had also struggled to integrate teacher assessment of National Curriculum levels with our school-based Records of Achievement which had been devised over a period of five years, following government initiatives to implement a national recording system. As if this was not complicated enough, the very language of the statements of attainment often failed to express the fine distinctions which needed to be made between one level and the next. Consider, for instance, what pupils were expected to demonstrate in statements of attainment 6a and 7a of Attainment Target 3: Writing:

> 6a) write in a variety of forms for a range of purposes, presenting subject matter differently to suit the needs of specified known audiences and demonstrating the ability to sustain the interest of the reader.
> 7a) write in a variety of forms, with commitment and a clear sense of purpose and awareness of audience, demonstrating an ability to anticipate the reader's response.

Is the 'range of purposes' mentioned in Level 6a but missing at Level 7 to be taken for granted at the later level? Why do the audiences have to be 'specified' and 'known' at Level 6 but not at Level 7? What is the difference between being able to 'sustain the interest of the reader' at Level 6 and 'demonstrating an ability to anticipate the reader's response' at Level 7? Such questions are difficult enough to answer in themselves; when applied to the assessment of pupils' writing they are almost impossible to resolve.

We were in the throes of carrying out standardizing exercises to help us to make judgements about such thorny issues when it became clear in early 1993 that the English National Curriculum was in the process of being revised. At the same time, the school was moving to a new pattern of communicating with parents which made it likely that our Record of Achievement system would be partly replaced by a more conventional method of reporting to meet the demands of Circular 14/92 (DFE 1992). Yet another internal change instigated by external prescription.

While all this was taking place, the department was: continuing to teach the General Certificate of Secondary Education (GCSE) Dual Certificate 100 per cent coursework syllabus to Year 11 for the last time in its comparatively short life-span; implementing Key Stage 4 through the new GCSE syllabus in Year 10; and anticipating that we would be required to submit a sample of pupils' coursework in Year 9 for the National Curriculum audit, as well as estimating a level in each of the Attainment Targets for each of our 270 pupils.

Where do we go from here?

By the time this chapter was completed in February 1994, Sir Ron Dearing, the chair of the School Curriculum and Assessment Authority (SCAA) had concluded his review of the content of the National Curriculum, the arrangements for testing, and the 10-level scale of children's attainment. The future, while appearing less bleak than when Dearing began his deliberations in April 1993, looks no less uncertain now than it did when Brian Cox was first commissioned to lead the National Curriculum working group for English in 1988. If there is optimism, it stems from the assurance that Dearing earnestly sought and responded to the views of teachers about the overloading of the assessment process and the time constraints within which the National Curriculum was being delivered. He appears too to understand the concerns about the use of crude data to assess the performance of schools and is aware of the need to balance continuous assessment in the classroom with testing outside it if children's progress is to be measured in a meaningful way.

However, a reconciliation between English teachers and their political masters is far from guaranteed. There is certainly much for the teaching profession to praise in the general recommendations which the Dearing Report makes. The National Curriculum is to be streamlined, offering schools increased choice of curriculum content and greater flexibility to structure their own time; teachers' work-load is to be reduced; there is to be a reduction in the prescription of what is taught, providing more scope for professional judge-ment; curriculum and assessment will be handled by one organiza-tion; record-keeping will be simplified; teacher assessment is to be reported to parents alongside SAT results; and there will be no further change to the National Curriculum for five years. All very welcome news indeed.

Yet, English teachers are finding the subject-specific recommen-dations less palatable. The SATs still remain in the new proposals, as they do for the other two core subjects – mathematics and science. While the time taken up by the English SATs has been reduced by half, the tiering system made more equitable and the Shakespeare text now made available to a wider audience, the fundamental objections to the SATs still remain: that they fail to assess in any meaningful way the kind of reading and writing responses which are integral to the process of teaching English in the classroom. In other words, they will still tell us little that we did not already know and, in many cases, may indicate considerably less.

At Key Stage 4, there will be confusion as parents and teachers struggle to compare pupils' progress with achievement at the previous Key Stage. The grading system for GCSE examinations will continue to be letters A–G, as the level 1–10 system will cease at the end of Key Stage 3. Examination boards had been instructed to retain the GCSE letter-based A–G scale for assessment purposes in the 1994 examinations while the Dearing review was carried out. Once again, of course, this is a double-edged sword. English teachers are now in their third term of teaching Year 10 GCSE pupils and have been assessing pupils' work on the 10-level scale. In any case, as Speaking and Listening (Attainment Target 1) is assessed solely by coursework and was never part of the A–G system, no grade criteria exist for it on the letter grade system. How this will be dealt with by the exam-ination boards remains to be seen. Further controversy is bound to be the result, not least because the 10-level scale does not convert easily back into A–G grades, particularly in the Level 7 area which straddles the crucial grade C/D borderline.

English teachers had hoped that Sir Ron Dearing would look again at GCSE and the present limit of 40 per cent on course work but, although the Report stressed that moderation procedures must not be excessively bureaucratic, the ceiling on course work remains at this figure. Despite the government's attempts to discredit the 1992 results, 100 per cent course work raised standards, improved pupil motiva-tion and led to imaginative syllabi and exciting school-based courses. It is because of this belief in the value of continuous assessment that a pressure group is recruiting ever-increasing support from English teachers who are demanding its return.

Most serious of all the objections is the Report's intention to use the Revised Orders in English, submitted to John Patten by the National Curriculum Council in September 1993, as the basis for the English subject group's deliberations on the slimming down of the English curriculum.

At the 1993 conference of the National Association of the Teaching of English, Henrietta Dombey, an early years specialist at the University of Brighton, argued cogently that, if the 10-level scale were to be revised, it must make sense to call for a postponement of the Revised English Orders. Brian Cox, at the same conference, went further in urging resistance to this document – and it is easy to see why. The National Curriculum Council's parting shot was to reduce English to a set of language skills in which form replaces content, and engagement with literature is overridden by an anxiety to analyse text. In the proposed new orders, Standard English is defined in terms of what is correct, both in speech and writing, and gone are references to knowledge about language and the media which gave teachers the means by which children could be encouraged to examine language as a social, living force. The retention of the 10-level scale of attainment at Key Stage 3, and the claim in the Dearing Report that this system works well in English precisely because of its hierarchical nature, gives rise to grave doubts about the framework within which English is intended to be taught. As Terry Furlong (1993), former chair of the National Association for the Teaching of English argues:

> There are . . . three dimensions of competence and ability in the use of the English language: knowledge, skills and understandings in and about language and its use; the range of materials, situations and contexts in which these can be applied; and the quality or effectiveness of the expression and the understanding in the context of its use. Only when these things are considered together, in a balanced and comprehensive way, can we come to some judgement about competence and ability . . . The Revised Orders attempt criteria only for the first aspect and even that is partial and incomplete . . . The system of levels and statements proposed in the re-written Order is an arbitrary set of subdivisions of a partial picture of competence.

Such emphasis on the mechanics of language is, in a more fundamental way than Cox's curriculum was, a major departure from the thinking of most, if not all, developments in English teaching since the Bullock Report (DES 1975).

So English teachers now stand at yet another crossroads. In the present climate it seems that there is only one certainty, however positive the potential outcome – change with its inevitable stress, as departments like mine once again modify teaching strategies, course content and assessment procedures to meet new demands.

It will, I think, be some time before English teachers are able to experience the sentiments and share the enthusiasm expressed by Robert Browning in the poem with which this chapter began.

POSTSCRIPT

Judith Bell

At the time this book was written, working parties were struggling with the unenviable task of interpreting the recommendations contained in the 1993 Dearing Report and producing guidelines for future practice. It will take some years before the full implications of the National Curriculum and its assessment procedures are fully implemented and workable systems devised. There is little doubt that reform was needed and perhaps the changes might not have been so Draconian if teachers had been more willing to compromise on some of the issues, though there is no evidence that the various Secretaries of State would have listened. Demands for greater accountability and better value for money are unlikely to diminish and no-one would argue against the view that money on education should be wisely spent.

Everyone – teachers, parents, governors, local education authorities and Secretaries of State – would agree that pupils and students are entitled to high quality education, but the speed with which reforms have been introduced and the persistent criticism of teaching standards have had a demoralizing effect on teachers, the vast majority of whom carry out their duties conscientiously and with a degree of commitment not generally appreciated by those on the outside.

There is little doubt the 'secret garden of the curriculum' is gone for ever, and teachers now acknowledge, albeit reluctantly in some cases, that for the foreseeable future, they will be required to teach within frameworks laid down by central government and that their professional autonomy will be limited. In Chapter 3, Karen Cowley writes:

> Undoubtedly professional autonomy was not a sufficient way of achieving public accountability. Nevertheless, a form of accountability which starts by totally undermining teaching autonomy is positively damaging. A better balance must be achieved between professional and economic accountability. In return for regaining a greater measure of autonomy over the core aspect of teaching, teachers must now expect to be evaluated against externally imposed criteria.

There are some hopeful signs for the future. If the implementation of the Dearing recommendations can be based on sound practice, then there is every chance that a workable system can be devised. Even so, it is likely to take many years and a great deal of good will before the impact of hastily introduced and often poorly thought out major reforms are forgotten. In the meantime, many able teachers have taken early or ill-health retirement – and no profession can afford to lose some of its most experienced workers.

REFERENCES

Apple, M. W. (1988). 'Work, class and teaching', in Ozga, J. (ed.) *Schoolwork; Approaches to the Labour Process of Teaching*. Milton Keynes, Open University Press.

Audit Commission (1993). *Adding up the Sums: Schools' Management of Their Finances*. London, HMSO.

Auld, Robin (1976). *William Tyndale Junior and Infants Schools Public Enquiry*. London, The Inner London Education Authority.

Ball, S. J. (1987). *The Micro-politics of the School*. London, Methuen.

Barker, B. (1986). *Rescuing the Comprehensive Experience*. Milton Keynes, Open University Press.

Becher, T. (1984). 'Principles and politics: an interpretative framework for university management', *International Journal of Institutional Management in Higher Education*, **8** (3), 191–9.

Becher, T. (1989). 'The national curriculum and the implementation gap', in Preedy, Margaret (ed.) *Approaches to Curriculum Management*. Milton Keynes, Open University Press.

Bennett, C. (1985). 'Paints, pots or promotion: art teachers' attitudes towards their careers', in Ball, S. J. and Goodson, I. F. (eds) *Teachers' Lives and Careers*. Lewes, Falmer Press.

Bevan, S. and Barber, L. (1994). *A Head for Figures*, Report No. 262. Institute of Manpower Studies, University of Sussex, Falmer, Brighton.

Bloom, B. (1976). *Human Characteristics and School Learning*. New York, McGraw-Hill.

Bolton, Eric (1993). Presidential address given at the North of England Education Conference.

Bunting, R. (1993). 'The importance of being well read', in *Language and Learning*, March 1993. Sheffield, National Association for the Teaching of English.

Cole, M. and Walker, S. (eds) (1989). *Teaching and Stress*. Milton Keynes, Open University Press.

Cooper, Cary L. and Kelly, Mike (1993). 'Occupational stress in head-teachers: a national UK study', *British Journal of Educational Psychology*, **63**, 130–43.

Cox, C. B. and Dyson, A. E. (1969). *Black Paper One: Fight for Education*. London, The Critical Quarterly Society.

Dale, R., Esland, G., Fergusson, R. and Macdonald, M. (eds) (1981). *Education and the State: Schooling and the National Interest*. Barcombe, Falmer Press.

Dearing, Sir Ron (1993). *The National Curriculum and its Assessment, Final Report*. London, School Curriculum and Assessment Authority.

Department for Education (DFE) (1991). *Education (School Teacher Appraisal) Regulations No. 1511*. London, HMSO.

Department for Education (1992). *Reports on Individual Pupils' Achievements, Circular 14/92*. London, HMSO.

Department for Education (1993). *School Governors: A Guide to the Law, County Controlled and Special Agreement Schools*. London, HMSO.

Department of Education and Science (DES) (1972). *Teacher Education and Training* (James Report). London, HMSO.

Department of Education and Science (1974). *Report of the Enquiry Into the Pay of Non-University Teachers* (Houghton Report), Cmnd 5848. London, HMSO.

Department of Education and Science (1975). *A Language for Life* (Bullock Report). London, HMSO.

Department of Education and Science (1977a). *Education in Schools: a consultative document, para. 1.5*, Cmnd 6869. London, HMSO.

Department of Education and Science (1977b). *A New Partnership for our Schools* (Taylor Report). London, HMSO.

Department of Education and Science (1985). *Better Schools*, Cmnd 9469. London, HMSO.

Department of Education and Science (1988a). *Education Reform Act: Local Management of Schools. Circular 7/88*. London, HMSO.

Department of Education and Science (1988b). *Report of the Committee of Enquiry into the Teaching of English Language* (Kingman Report). London, HMSO.

Department of Education and Science (1988c). *School Governors: A Guide to the Law, County and Controlled Schools*. London, HMSO.

Department of Education and Science (1989). *English for Ages 5–16* (Cox Report). London, HMSO.

Department of Education and Science (1990). *English in the National Curriculum*. London, HMSO.

Evans, M. A. (1991). 'Personal reflections on headship', in Mortimore, P. and Mortimore, J. (eds) *Secondary Headship: Roles, Responsibilities and Reflections*. London, Paul Chapman.

Fitch, Sir Joshua (1865). Quoted in Bryan, K. A. (1969). The Educational Works of Sir Joshua Fitch. Unpublished MA thesis, University of Wales.

Freedman, S. (1988). 'Teacher "burnout" and institutional stress', in Ozga, J. (ed.) Schoolwork: approaches to the Labour Process of Teaching. Milton Keynes, Open University Press.

Furlong, T. (1993). 'Learning without words: a response to Dearing', The English and Media Magazine, 29, Autumn.

Gipps, C. and Stobart, S. (1993). Assessment: a Teacher's Guide to the Issues. Sevenoaks, Hodder and Stoughton.

Grace, G. (1987). 'Teachers and the State in Britain: a Changing Relation', in Lawn, M. and Grace G. (eds) Teachers: the culture and politics of work. Lewes, Falmer Press.

Haigh, G. (1993). 'Entrance and exit', The Times Educational Supplement, 5 February, R10.

Hargreaves, A. and Fullan, M. G. (eds) (1992). Understanding Teacher Development. London, Cassell.

Harris, S. (1992). 'A Career on the Margins? The position of careers teachers in schools', British Journal of Sociology of Education, 13 (2), 163–76.

Hilsum, S. and Start, K. R. (1974). Promotion and Careers in Teaching. Windsor, NFER.

Hoyle, E. (1986). The Politics of School Management. Sevenoaks, Hodder and Stoughton.

Huberman, M. (1993). The Lives of Teachers. London, Cassell.

Hughes, E. C. (1937). 'Institutional office and the person', in Hughes, E. C. (1958). Men and Their Work. New York, Free Press.

Hughes, E. C. (1958). Men and Their Work. New York, Free Press.

Jones, A. (1987). Leadership for Tomorrow's Schools. Oxford, Blackwell.

Jung, C. (1926). 'The structure and dynamics of the psyche', in Collected Works, Vol. 8. Princeton NJ, Princeton University Press.

Kyriacou, C. (1989). 'The nature and prevalence of teacher stress', in Cole, M. and Walker, S. (eds) Teaching and Stress. Milton Keynes, Open University Press.

Lancashire County Council (1990). Scheme for the Local Management of Schools in Lancashire. Preston, Lancashire County Council.

Lawley, P. (1988). Deputy Headship. Harlow, Longman.

Levinson, D. J., Darrow, C. N., Klein, G. B., Levinson, M. H. and McKee, B. (1978). The Seasons of a Man's Life. New York, Knopf.

Local Management in Schools Initiative (1988). Local Management in Schools: A Practical Guide. London, The Local Management in Schools Initiative.

Lyons, G. (1981). Teacher Careers and Career Perceptions. Windsor, NFER-Nelson.

Lyons, G. and McCleary, L. (1980). 'Careers in teaching', in Hoyle, E. and Megarry, J. (eds) World Yearbook of Education 1980: the Professional Development of Teachers. London, Kogan Page.

McIntyre, A. (1989). 'Evaluating schools in the context of the Education Reform Act', in Preedy, M. (ed.) Approaches to Curriculum Management. Milton Keynes, Open University Press.

Maclean, R. (1992). Teachers' Careers and Promotion Patterns: a Sociological Analysis. Lewes, Falmer Press.

Maclure, S. (1988). *Education Reformed: a Guide to the Education Reform Act 1988*. Sevenoaks, Hodder and Stoughton.

Morgan, C., Hall, V. and Mackay, H. (1983). *The Selection of Secondary School Headteachers*. Milton Keynes, Open University Press.

Morgan, C., Hall, V. and Mackay, H. (1986). *Headteachers at Work*. Milton Keynes, Open University Press.

National Commission on Education (November 1993). *Learning to Succeed. Report of the enquiry chaired by Lord Walton of Detchant*. London, Heinemann.

National Curriculum Council (NCC) (1990). *Careers Education and Guidance, Curriculum Guidance 6*. York, NCC.

National Curriculum Council (1992). *National Curriculum English: The Case for Revising the Order*. York, NCC.

Office for Standards in Education (OFSTED) (1993). *Standards and Quality in Education 1992–93. The Annual Report of Her Majesty's Chief Inspector of Schools*. London, HMSO.

Rutter, M., Maughan, B., Mortimore, P. and Ouston, J. (1979). *1500 Hours*. Shepton Mallet, Open Books.

School Examinations and Assessment Council (SEAC) (1992). *Key Stage 3: School Assessment Folder: Information on the 1993 Tests: English*. London, HMSO.

Sikes, P. J., Measor, L. and Woods, P. (1985). *Teacher Careers: Crises and Continuities*. Lewes, Falmer Press.

Smith, D. and Tomlinson, S. (1989). *The School Effect*. London, Policy Studies Institute.

Spencer, A. (1989). 'Building effective relationships between teachers and LEA subject advisers', in Preedy, M. (ed.) (1989), *Teachers' Case Studies in Educational Management*. London, Paul Chapman.

Task Group on Assessment and Testing (TGAT) (1988). *The National Curriculum: A Report*. London, Department of Education and Science and the Welsh Office.

Thomas, N. (1982). 'HM Inspectorate', in McCormick, R. and Nuttall, D. L. (eds) *Curriculum Evaluation, and Assessment in Educational Institutions*, Part 3, Block 2 of Open University course E364. Milton Keynes, Open University Press.

Travers, C. J. and Cooper, C. L. (1991). 'Stress and status in teaching: an investigation of potential gender-related relationships', *Women in Management Review and Abstracts*, **6** (4), 16–23, MCB University Press, 0955–8357.

Unwin, L. (1993). 'Training credits: the pilot doomed to succeed', in Richardson, W., Woolhouse, J. and Finegold, D. (eds) *The Reform of Post-16 Education and Training*. London, Longman.

Walker, S. and Barton, L. (eds) (1987). *Changing Policies, Changing Teachers: New Directions for Schooling?* Milton Keynes, Open University Press.

Walsh, K. (1987). 'The politics of teacher appraisal' in Lawn, M. and Grace, G. (eds) *Teachers: The Culture and Politics of Work*. Lewes, Falmer Press.

Watts, T. (1994). 'Careers must not be overlooked', *The Times Educational Supplement*, 11 February 1994.

Wragg, E. (1988). *Education in the Market Place: the Ideology Behind the Education Reform Act 1988*. London, National Union of Teachers.

INDEX

accountability, 19–22, 24–9
Apple (1988), 17
appraisal, 66–7
Audit Commission (1993), 82
Auld (1976), 4
autonomy, 3, 13–29

Bachelor of Education (BEd), 34–7
Ball (1987), 53, 56
Barker (1986), 17
Becher (1984), 56
Becher (1989), 7
Bennett (1985), 42, 53
Better Schools (DES 1985), 17
Bevan and Barber (1994), 82
Bloom (1976), 26
Bolton (1993), 6–9
Bullock Report (DES 1975), 111, 121
Bunting (1993), 114
burnout, 17, 51–2

careers education, 8, 101–9
Certificate of Secondary Education, 5, 20

classroom discipline, 11, 35–6, 70–8
Cole and Walker (1989), 9
control, 13–18, 19–29, 111
Cooper and Kelly (1993), 9, 10
Cox, B., 113, 121
Cox and Dyson (1969a), 111
Cox Report (DES 1989a), 113

Dale et al. (1981), 77
Dearing, Sir Ron and Dearing (1993), 11–12, 17, 25, 119–20, 123–4
Department for Education
  1991 (Education (School Teacher Appraisal) regulations), 27
  1992 (Circular 14/92), 119
  1993 (School Governors: A Guide to the Law), 95
Department of Education and Science
  1972 (James Report), 43
  1974 (Houghton Report), 13, 42

DOING YOUR RESEARCH PROJECT (2nd edition)
A GUIDE FOR FIRST-TIME RESEARCHERS IN
EDUCATION AND SOCIAL SCIENCE
Judith Bell

If you are a beginner researcher, the problems facing you are much the same
whether you are producing a small project, an MEd dissertation or a PhD
thesis. You will need to select a topic; identify the objectives of your study;
plan and design a suitable methodology; devise research instruments; nego-
tiate access to institutions, material and people; collect, analyse and present
information; and finally, produce a well-written report or dissertation. Whatever the scale of the undertaking, you will have to master techniques and
devise a plan of action which does not attempt more than the limitations of
expertise, time and access permit.

We all learn to do research by actually doing it, but a great deal of time can
be wasted and goodwill dissipated by inadequate preparation. This book
aims to provide you with the tools to do the job, to help you avoid some
of the pitfalls and time-wasting false trails that can eat into your time, to
establish good research habits, and to take you from the stage of choosing
a topic through to the production of a well-planned, methodologically sound
and well-written final report or dissertation on time.

Doing Your Research Project serves as a source of reference and guide to good
practice for all beginner researchers, whether undergraduate and postgraduate students or professionals such as teachers or social workers undertaking
investigations in Education and the Social Sciences. This second edition re-
tains the basic structure of the very successful first edition whilst incorporating some important new material.

Contents
*Introduction – Approaches to educational research – Planning the project – Keeping
records and making notes – Reviewing the literature – Negotiating access and the
problems of inside research – The analysis of documentary evidence – Designing
and administering questionnaires – Planning and conducting interviews – Diaries
– Observation studies – Interpretation and presentation of the evidence – Postscript
– References – Index.*

192pp   0 335 19094 4 (Paperback)

WORKING AND LEARNING TOGETHER FOR CHANGE

Colin Biott and Jennifer Nias (eds)

This book gives practitioners a voice through accounts of a wide range of shared work and learning. There are chapters on pre-service, in-service and adult education, as well as a particularly thought-provoking section on learning and change from a feminist perspective. Overall, the book offers teachers and teacher educators detailed examples of collaborative relationships and possible models for professional development. It provides descriptions of and approaches to teacher development which enable individuals, working with challenging peers, to examine critically their assumptions and actions, and to try out and evaluate alternatives. It is written by practitioners who have worked and learned with others and who have distilled from that experience the ways in which it has contributed to change within themselves, within their groups and within their institutions. Their stories do not suggest that professional change is swiftly or easily accomplished even within the context of collaborative activity. All the accounts describe it as a difficult and painful but also as a satisfying and ultimately worthwhile process. They demonstrate that teachers and teacher educators can enter into and sustain effective partnerships which lead to changes in educational systems and processes.

Contents

Contributors

Kate Ashcroft, Sheena Ball, Colin Biott, Penelope Campbell, Andy Convery, Sue Gollop, Mary Heath, Jay Mawdsley, Jennifer Nias, Anne Spendiff, Robin Yeomans.

176pp   0 335 09716 2 (Paperback)   0 335 09717 0 (Hardback)

MANAGING CHANGE IN SCHOOLS

Patrick Whitaker

Schools are currently undergoing a period of upheaval and change as they adapt to new requirements and altered circumstances. This phase of rapid and accelerating change is a characteristic of organizational life as we move towards the twenty-first century and it presents novel and unprecedented challenges to those charged with the management of schools.

The book sets out to explore the world of change in which education is now set. It explores the changed and changing environment to which teachers are having constantly to respond and adapt and examines the personal, professional and organizational implications involved. The book proposes that a major shift in our management thinking is necessary if the emerging challenges to education are to be met successfully. The book will offer frameworks for considering the management of change, outline the professional learning necessary and provide practical strategies for management development.

It is comforting and refreshing to come across an education writer who is prepared to tell heads to slow down and pause for thought ... Whitaker's book is also applicable to anyone who is in a leadership position in a school at any level. Indeed, a core theme of this book is the idea that leadership rather than management is the most crucial focus for the development of our schools in the years ahead ... Books about the management of change in schools are all too abundant, but good ones are rare. Patrick Whitaker has written one of the best.

(Tony Mooney, *Times Educational Supplement*)

Contents

Introduction – Preface – The educational context – Perspectives on change – The personal dimension – The dynamics of change – Leadership and change – Organizational cultures – Frameworks and strategies for change – Challenges for the future – Bibliography – Index.

176pp   0 335 09381 7 (Paperback)